SELF-PORTRAIT

So we beat on, boats against the current, borne back ceaselessly into the past.

F. SCOTT FITZGERALD
The Great Gatsby

SELF-PORTRAIT:
Ceaselessly Into The Past

ROSS MACDONALD

Foreword by Eudora Welty

Edited and with an Afterword by Ralph B. Sipper

CAPRA *PRESS*
1981
Santa Barbara

Cover illustration by Kathleen Mackintosh.
Back cover photograph, courtesy of Ross Macdonald.

Library of Congress Cataloging in Publication Data
Macdonald, Ross, 1915-
Self-portrait, ceaselessly into the past.
1. Millar, Kenneth, 1915- —Biography—
Addresses, essays, lectures. 2. Novelists,
American—20th century—Biography—Addresses,
essays, lectures. I. Sipper, Ralph B.
II. Title
PS3525.I486Z47   813'.52 (B)   81-10258
ISBN 0-88496-170-2   AACR2
ISBN 0-88496-169-9 (pbk.)

CAPRA PRESS
Post Office Box 2068
Santa Barbara, CA 93120

CONTENTS

FOREWORD

Eudora Welty

KENNETH MILLAR did not sit down and write an autobiography as such; it has arrived of itself, in its own time, and is an accretion—a circumstance that seems characteristic of this modest and meditative man. It is an autobiography, though—by virtue of occasional essays, introductions and prefaces to fiction, his own and others', and to a bibliography another prepared of his work. One foreword begins: "Most fiction is shaped by geography and permeated by autobiography, even when it is trying not to be." If the autobiographical content of what follows has been obliquely provided, it is not oblique itself. When this writer's concentrated gaze does take in himself, it is direct and central. What we have is the clear, the clarified, result of long thoughts. The ordinary autobiography is designed to give more information, but we are not begrudged here of something better; we are quietly offered not details but essences.

Major factors emerge: how the sea became, very early, the most deeply felt element in Ken Millar's life; how the sense of family became the generative force of his work and its true subject, not by way of a happy and secure childhood but through the uncertainties of being moved about constantly during his formative years, of knowing very young the unsettled lives of his parents, and the father's desertion of the home. We learn that his belonging by birth and by his raising in two different countries brought him, through his own deliberate struggling with it, to the profound and liberating recognition of what place meant. We find how the same migrations planted in that lively and curious mind a lifelong interest in the North American *colloquial* language, which became the closely studied instrument of his work.

Customarily, he brings up a fact of his life in order to clarify a point about the craft of writing. He thus remarks in the course of the excellent introduction he provided for Matthew J. Bruccoli's bibliography of his work: "The year I graduated

i

(from high school), 1932, I counted the rooms I had lived in during my first sixteen years, and got a total of fifty"—to go on: "Novelists are made, if they are made at all, out of uncertain beginnings and long delayed completions, like their books." Of the writing of his "break-through" novel, *The Galton Case*, he says, "I approached my life from a distance, and crept up on it in disguise as one might track an alien enemy; the details of the book were all invented. But there was personal truth in its broad shape."

It occurs to me that this book with its personal truths might be more strictly thought of as a self-portrait. Reading the succeeding pieces, you are really allowed to see the author not in time stages but all at once. You see him writing what he has written over the years. Most self-portraits are painted by their artists with the aid of mirrors; a writer's work may reflect him only in part, but here, when he looks into it himself and knowingly, it shows him to his reader in a curious, and affecting, doubling of honesty.

The portrait is complex in a still further respect. There is the writer, and there is the private person; and there is also a third, Archer. The essay which tells of the relationship between them is an astonishing achievement in self-perception. The most significant fact in the close alliance between a writer's life and his fiction (however close, or however far apart, they might on surface appear) lies in his art, continuous and developing, of making one out of the other. Not surprisingly, the father figure appears in roles of significance in most Macdonald novels (as he appears in the Millar essays). A principle in the novels is that what was missing reappears— people, information, evidence, old crimes, buried victims, sometimes lost love. Solution is found when, and where, relationships reach full circle. It is human relationships that must be sought for, discovered, and at last understood.

Ken Millar had learned that for himself intensity of feeling, if it is to become accessible in fiction's terms, requires distancing, requires the perspective that comes of precise observation and of irony. This is one of the marks of his seriousness as a writer which makes so valuable what he can tell us about the crime novel. *As* this serious writer, he has respected the form, and has respected it best by making it his own. He is, as we know, its master: it responds to a very broad range of his powers.

We keep in mind his own work in the context of the essay written to introduce his *Great Stories of Suspense,* his brilliant analysis of the function and place of the crime novel, its form, its history, its relation to other branches of the novel, its significance in our national culture. In particular we can realize their force as a reflection of the life of our day. Just as Wilkie Collins's *The Woman in White* with "its dark and knowing look at Victorian society," remains a living portrait of Collins's England, *The Far Side of the Dollar, The Zebra-Striped Hearse, Black Money, The Underground Man* and other equally compelling Macdonald novels will continue to give back to their future readers the life, to its most sensitive fluctuations, of his changing California.

In the portrait yet another profile is to be traced in the eloquent introduction to Robert Easton's account of the tragedy of the Santa Barbara Oil Spill of 1969. Ken Millar's passionate and always active concern for the conservation of the natural world is vividly clear here. Of course, all his fiction too is shot through with his love for this beautiful world of mountain and sea where he lives. (I shall never forget his showing it to me.)

The spoilers of the natural world are also the spoilers of the innocent and vulnerable; his crime novels connect them in ways that reach far and far back. That same 1969 oil spill is the explosive force in his fine novel *Sleeping Beauty,* where it is given the full strength of his tragic insight into its human motivation, its pattern of family connection. One speaks to him of the other: the mistreatment of the natural world and the damage people do to their fellow human beings. Violence is all one language—or rather the same lack, deprivation, of any other language. One of the gentlest of men, Ken Millar has not found the basilisk face of evil to be inscrutable.

The superb dramatic structure he gives his novels carries full weight of their social implications; his suspenseful plots are vehicles of moral suspense. The intensity of his human concern has found its form, so suited to his demands and so perfectly controlled, because he is the gifted writer he is, and the kind of writer he is.

iii

Introducing the 1979 trilogy *Archer in Jeopardy*, he writes: "The underlying theme of these three novels, as I read them now, is the migration of a mind from one place and culture to another. Its purpose, like the dominant purpose of my young life, was to repossess my American birthplace by imaginative means . . . In the end I possess my birthplace and am possessed by its language."

This is a poet's concept too. In a recent essay, Seamus Heany, who is also of two cultures, writes: "Certainly the secret of being a poet, Irish or otherwise, lies in the summoning of the energies of words. But my quest for definition, while it may lead backward, is conducted in the living speech of the landscape I was born into. If you like, I began as a poet when my roots were crossed with my reading."

What this imaginative novelist has learned from his own migrations, what he retains indelibly in his memory, that long memory, what he continues through the changing times to learn and observe, examine—all, in the sea-change of fiction writing, appear, are resurrected, in the invention of character, and in the development with all the brilliant Macdonald complexities, convolutions, and stunning surprises, of plot. All this has come, and more will surely continue to come, out of what he calls in one essay "the inner shape of a man's life," which itself "remains as personal and hidden as his skeleton, just as intricate, almost as unchangeable."

One most important element in both the life of the writer and the writer's work, and one that closely connects them, binds them together indissolubly, has to do with his creation of the style by which we know him—I think it is the best way we do know him. But this is not one of the subjects that lends itself to words of discussion, much less revelation—it is not a subject for any autobiography. We can only observe that style lies very close to a writer's life, and in the completest way allows the writer's work to speak to us.

As it does here.

We are grateful for this book. One further thing about Ken Millar's kind of autobiography: it is open-ended. There will always be room for more, when the time is right and the inclination takes hold. As it now stands, it is a valuable and moving document of a most valuable man.

SELF-PORTRAIT

1

Down These Streets
a Mean Man Must Go

I ONCE COMPARED the detective story to a welder's mask which enables both writer and reader to handle dangerously hot materials. For even at its least realistic crime fiction reminds us of real things. The world is a treacherous place, it says, where a man must learn to watch his step and guard his rights. It is a difficult place to know; still, both the natural and the human worlds are subject to certain laws which we can understand rationally and make predictions by. Traditional detective fiction offers us the assurance that in spite of all its horrors—the speckled band in Conan Doyle, the dead girl thrust up the chimney in Poe's *Rue Morgue*—the world makes sense and can be understood.

Poe lived out in his short brilliant career the last days of the age of reason and the descent into the maelstrom of the unconscious, where everything revolved at a new angle. It was with a kind of desperation—a desperation we continue to feel—that he held on to rational explanations. The murdered girl in the chimney, Dupin assures us, was only the victim of an animal. But in spite of this explanation the story leaves a residue of horror. The forces of terror and reason remain in unresolved conflict.

In the following century that conflict became the central feature of the detective story. Explaining fears which can't quite be explained away, transforming nightmares into daymares, it helped to quiet the nerves and satisfy the minds of countless readers.

Poe's master Coleridge had written of the Gothic romance, the precursor of the modern detective story:

"As far, therefore, as the story is concerned, the praise which a romance can claim, is simply that of having given pleasure during its perusal . . . .To this praise, however, our author has not entitled himself. The sufferings which he describes are so frightful and intolerable, that we break with abruptness from the delusion and indignantly suspect the man of a species of brutality . . . . Let him work *physical* wonders only, and we will be content to dream with him for a while; but the first *moral* miracle which he attempts, he disgusts and awakens us . . . how beings like ourselves would feel and act . . . our own feelings sufficiently instruct us; and we instantly reject the clumsy fiction that does not harmonize with them."

This is as you may recognize from a review of Lewis's *The Monk* written by Coleridge in 1796, the year that he began to compose *The Ancient Mariner.* It is worth quoting not just for its associations but because it can remind us that the Gothic tradition goes back at least as far as the eighteenth century, and its basic rule hasn't changed radically since. The moral life of the characters is the essence of the story, authenticated by the moral life of the reader.

It was not just as a critic that Coleridge was interested in Gothic romance. *The Ancient Mariner* was touched by it, and the unfinished *Christabel* might almost be described as a Gothic novel in verse. Perhaps I am old enough to confess publicly what forty years ago was my secret ambition. When I was a young would-be poet going to school at the University of Western Ontario, I planned to finish *Christabel* and made an attempt which fortunately doesn't survive, indeed it was stillborn. With the shocking realization of my limitations, my ambition split into two divergent parts which I have spent most of my life trying to put together again. I migrated to Ann Arbor and wrote a dissertation on the psychological backgrounds of Coleridge's criticism. At the same time I followed my wife's example and began to write mystery stories.

For a long time I was made to feel by my friends and colleagues that these two departments of my mental life, the

4

scholarly and the popular, were rather schizophrenically at odds with each other. Most of my best friends are fiction writers and scholars—most of my enemies, too. The writers viewed my interest in scholarship with suspicion not untinged with superstitious awe. The scholars—with significant exceptions like Marshall MacLuhan and Hugh Kenner—considered my fiction writing a form of prostitution out of which they tried to wrestle my soul. But I persisted in my intellectual deviance, trying to stretch my legs to match Chandler's markings, telling myself that down these streets a mean man must go.

It may be timely—I may not have another chance—to offer for the record some further autobiographical fragments and a few conclusions. The connections between the work and the life—other men's as well as my own—have always interested me. It becomes more and more evident that novels, popular or otherwise, are built like Robinson Crusoe's cabin out of the flotsam of the author's past and his makeshift present. A man's fiction, no matter how remote it may seem to be from the realistic or the autobiographical, is very much the record of his particular life. Gradually it may tend to become a substitute for the life, a shadow of the life clinging to the original so closely that (as in Malcolm Lowry's *Under the Volcano*) it becomes hard to tell which is fiction and which is confession.

As a writer grows older more and more of his energy goes to sustain the shadow. He seems to live primarily in order to go on writing, secondarily in order to have something to write about. This double *modus vivendi* is like that of an aging husband and wife each of whom knows what the other is going to say, and it often issues in stretching silences. Then we turn back in memory to the past, where the crucial events and conversations of our lives repeat themselves forever in the hope of being understood and perhaps forgiven.

I was born near San Francisco in 1915. My father and his father were both Scots-Canadian newspaper editors. There are writers and painters in my mother's family. My father left my mother when I was four. To me he ultimately bequeathed his copy of *Walden* and a life insurance policy for two thousand dollars which in Canada, in the thirties, was exactly enough to see me through four years of University.

Before I reached University, looking for something to become in my father's absence, I had become a writer. I think most fiction writers must suffer some degree of alienation, a suppression of the conative by the cognitive which stands like a reflecting window between them and the actual world of satisfactions. We wish to reach and remake that world symbolically, sometimes out of anger and revenge, sometimes out of a humane desire to reclaim it.

When I was eleven I discovered *Oliver Twist* and read that novel with such intense absorption that my mother feared for my health. She took the book away and sent me outside to play hockey. The scene was Kitchener, Ontario, a main source of talent for the National Hockey League. I fell on the ice and got my face cut by the skate of my friend Wilbert Hiller, who not many years later was playing for the New York Rangers. Thus I acquired my wound.

I seem to have got the makings of my bow at the Kitchener Public Library. The librarian, B. Mabel Dunham, was a novelist whose books are still alive though she is not. At least one of her novels was about the migration of the Pennsylvania Dutch to Canada in the nineteenth century. My mother's people, like Miss Dunham's were Pennsylvania Dutch; I must be the only American crime novelist who got his early ethical training in a Canadian Mennonite Sunday School. I believe that Mabel Dunham's living example, combined with the books both English and American with which she stocked the public library, permitted me to think of becoming a writer. By my middle teens I was a practising crime writer, and my high school classmate and future wife Margaret had begun to write in the Gothic vein, too. I have often wondered why. Perhaps we both felt that with the suppression of the personal and emotional life which afflicted Canada, particularly in those depression years, expressions of the angry self had to come out in devious ways.

What were we angry about? I think it may have been our sense of being provincial in a double sense, in relation to both Great Britain and the United States. My own feeling of distance from the center was deepened by the fact that I had been born in California and was an American citizen by birth. *Civis Romanus sum.*

Popular fiction is not generally thought of as autobiographical—it is considered less a person than a thing—and it is true

6

that the popular conventions offer an apparent escape from both the author's and the reader's lives. But in a deeper sense they can offer the writer a mask for autobiography—a fencer's mask to deflect the cold steel of reality as he struggles with his own Falstaffian shadows. The convention provides means of disguising the authorial self, but that self reappears on other levels in the forms of other characters, and as the Hamlet's cloud on which the whole thing is projected.

I can think of few more complex critical enterprises than disentangling the mind and life of a first-person detective story writer from the mask of his detective-narrator. The assumption of the mask is as public as vaudeville but as intensely private as a lyric poem. It is like taking an alias, the alias John Doe or Richard Roe; and it constitutes among other things an act of identification with the people one is writing for. Sam Spade is both Hammett and Hammett's audience, a Janus figure representing a city.

Hammett's books were not in the thirties to be found on the open shelves of the Kitchener Public Library. Neither were the novels of Hemingway, Faulkner, or Flaubert: as I recorded in my own early novel *Blue City,* these masters were kept in a locked cupboard for posterity. But one day in 1930 or 1931 I found *The Maltese Falcon* on the shelf of a lending library in a Kitchener tobacco shop, and I read a good part of it on the spot. It wasn't escape reading. As I stood there absorbing Hammett's novel, the slot machines at the back of the shop were clanking and whirring, and in the billiard room upstairs the perpetual poker game was being played. Like iron filings magnetized by the book in my hands, the secret meanings of the city began to organize themselves around me like a second city.

For the first time that I can remember I was consciously experiencing in my own sensibility the direct meeting of art and contemporary actuality—an experience that popular art at its best exists to provide—and beginning to find a language and a shape for that experience. It was a long time before I got it into writing, even crudely: *Blue City* was written fifteen years later. And it was much later still, long after I had made my way back to California and realized that the work of writers like Hammett and Chandler was as much my heritage as anyone's, that I wrote a detective novel called *The Galton Case,* about the

7

reclamation of a California birthright. I was forty or so, and it was getting very late. I made an all-out effort to bend the bow that Hammett and Chandler, and Mabel Dunham, had strung for me, and to hit the difficult target of my own life.

Most popular writers seem to begin, as I did, by imitating their predecessors. There is a convention to be learned. It keeps the forms of the art alive for both the writer and his readers, endowing both with a common stock of structural shapes and formal possibilities. A popular work like Mrs. Radcliffe's *Mysteries of Udolpho*, which incidentally Coleridge gave a better review than he gave Monk Lewis's book, prepares the ground for a *Northanger Abbey*, possibily even for a *Christabel*. The story line of Coleridge's unfinished poem, if not its subtle content, had its sources in several popular modes, including the Gothic tales of terror and the ballads, as well as in the terrible dreams that shook Coleridge nightly.

I believe that popular culture is not and need not be at odds with high culture, any more than the rhythms of walking are at odds with the dance. Popular writers learn what they can from the masters; and even the masters may depend on the rather sophisticated audience and the vocabulary of shapes and symbols which popular fiction provides. Without the traditional Gothic novel and its safety net of readers, even Henry James could not have achieved the wire-walking assurance with which he wrote *The Turn of the Screw*. The work which T.S. Eliot considered the next step taken after James by the Anglo-American novel, *The Great Gatsby*, has obvious connections with American crime fiction and the revolution effected in that fiction during the twenties. The skeleton of Fitzgerald's great work, if not its nervous system, is that of a mystery novel.

A functioning popular literature appears to be very useful if not essential to the growth of a higher literature. Chandler's debt to Fitzgerald suggests that the reverse is also true. There is a two-way connection between the very greatest work and the anonymous imaginings of a people.

I don't intend to suggest that popular literature is primarily a matrix for higher forms. Popular fiction, popular art in general, is the very air a civilization breathes. (Air itself is 80 percent nitrogen.) Popular art is the form in which a culture comes to be known by most of its members. It is the carrier and guardian of

8

the spoken language. A book which can be read by everyone, a convention which is widely used and understood in all its variations, holds a civilization together as nothing else can.

It reaffirms our values as they change, and dramatizes the conflicts of those values. It absorbs and domesticates the spoken language, placing it in meaningful context with traditional language, forming new linguistic synapses in the brain and body of the culture. It describes new modes of behavior, new versions of human character, new shades and varieties of good and evil, and implicitly criticizes them. It holds us still and contemplative for a moment, caught like potential shoplifters who see their own furtive images in a scanning mirror, and wonder if the store detective is looking.

2

A Collection of Reviews

On the morning of December 13, 1915, a man who had never seen Scotland sat down at his desk in a California town and wrote a Scots dialect poem in something like the manner of Bobby Burns. The poem began:

> *December's glaur was thick the morn*
> *That Jock and Nanny's bairn was born.*
> *His name was Kenneth.*

Jock was my father John Millar. Nanny was my mother Ann. The bairn of course was I. Having completed the poem, my father took it down the street to the offices of the Los Gatos newspaper and offered it for publication. It was cheerfully accepted. My father and the editor were friends: both were printers as well as writers, and the poem celebrating my birth was soon in print.

My father and mother were forty years old at the time, and had returned from a difficult assignment in the Northwest Territories, on the shores of Great Slave Lake. There my father had started a small government-supported newspaper, and my mother, who was a graduate of Winnipeg General Hospital, set up a nursing station. But they had retreated at least temporarily to California.

Both of their early lives had been intensely active. My father had been a swimmer and wrestler, once winner of the two-mile swim across Colpoys Bay; a man of middle size who could lift a half-ton weight. Before he was out of his teens he was teaching school, and beginning to write. Writing came naturally to him. His father was the founding editor of the local weekly, *The Walkerton Herald*, and a literate Glasgow Scot. But I somehow doubt that my father was wholly at ease with his father.

At any rate he had come west again and taken up some of his earlier interests. Supporting himself as a harbor pilot in and out of Vancouver Harbor, and living with my mother and me in a waterfront hotel, he resumed the pursuits that had in the first place drawn him west. He had long since become familiar with the Indians of Vancouver Island and the mainland, and with the artists (like John Innes) who were painting them. My father's interests ranged into other fields, and focused on the west coast Japanese. According to the family mythology (which in this case seemed to be true), when the young Mackenzie King came out to the coast to study the Japanese and other groups, my father was one of his consultants.

I was on the scene myself in a year or two, and recording fragments of those far-off days. I haven't forgotten the childish embarrassment I suffered when I spilled black ink on a Japanese gentleman's writing pad, but I remember the courtesy he showed me, sixty years ago, on the far edge of my life. Quite suddenly, I began to notice more public events, culminating in the marching and the cheering in the Vancouver streets which signalled the end of the war. One of those days still seems the happiest day of my childhood if not my life. I mean the unforgettable day when my father first took me to sea in a harbor boat, and I stood beside him in the offshore light, with his hands and my hand on the wheel.

Not all of the adventures I shared with my father were serious. He had lost most of his hair by the time I was born, and in my earliest memories of him he was totally bald. He bought a red wig matching his coloring, but soon grew weary of it. I inherited the wig, and the streets of downtown Vancouver were haunted for a while by a three-year-old midget with shaggy red hair.

It was a time of relief for most of the western world, but not for my mother. Though she had lived in large cities like Chicago, she remained at heart an Ontario farmer's daughter. I think

12

she had grown weary of hotels and the changing lives of their occupants, weary of even gentle people like Mrs. Swinkels, who lived just down the hall and sometimes talked of her days as a lady in waiting to the Queen of Holland. Such grandiose myths or memories only set in relief the problems of the present. My father changed place too often, and spent too much time on what my mother considered his hobbies. He would pass half the morning explaining Indian signs to a casual visitor, or while away the night listening to the Klondike veteran who lived in a basement room of our hotel. The veteran's name was Joe Brewer, and he gave me the hunting knife with which he claimed he had once fought off a grizzly bear. The knife was there to prove it, and I believed him. So did my father, I think. My mother didn't. And when even the Great War had ended, her private war with the two men continued.

Not long after the impromptu marching in the streets that marked the end of the war, my parents separated. My mother took me to her home territory in Ontario, and from then on I lived mostly with her and her people. But throughout my life I remained my father's son, even though I saw him infrequently, sometimes not for years at a time. He grew ill and prematurely old. When he returned from his absences, his decline was underlined, sometimes very sharply, as if he had aged five years in as many weeks. I grew afraid of losing him entirely. But east and west he traveled, still on the trail of a wished-for world where Indians and white men shared the unploughed territories or climbed through the blowing passes to the north. Though my father's life was more adventurous, and less prosperous, I became aware at almost every turn that it was patterned on *his* father's life, just as my own recurrences to the west and north have been patterned on my father's.

His younger sister Margaret had become for a while the center of the family, at least for me. She was a business woman in Manitoba, and for two years she kept me in a Winnipeg boarding school. My father came to visit his sister and me on his last trip out of the far west. He was smiling but uncertain, not only of me and his sister but of the world. I loved him still (though I faulted him perhaps unfairly for leaving me years ago) but I was unable to commit myself to his uncertain life. I was eleven years old, just starting my high school years, and there was nothing I could do for my father except think of him, as I still do, with love and sorrow.

I stayed in the Winnipeg boarding school and spent the weekends with my aunt. She was a generous aunt and it was a good school; I was grateful for their protection. In my second year there, I took some scholastic prizes and spent a lot of time in the gymnasium. My father had finally gone back to his home territory in Ontario, to Walkerton and the Bruce Peninsula where I had spent earlier years with his cousin Rob. If I was inclined to believe in conspiracies, I might have come to believe that someone, perhaps my mother's family, had conspired to keep my father and me apart. But I think it was more blind accident, my father's illness and my childish inability to govern my own life. Still I felt guilty. It seemed that he had left me when I was young and helpless, now I was leaving him in his helpless age. And I wonder if the Bruce Peninsula still fosters these long conspiracies of silent pain.

My father came close to ending his days on a rundown Bruce Peninsula farm with a sick male cousin. My father had lost the power of speech but was still able to write. When I visited him and his cousin he sat smiling up at me, propped by pillows, in the middle of the ruined farm, and showed me what he had been writing. His eyes were alive with it, shining in contrast with the dull dead eyes of his cousin.

The last time I saw my father's living eyes, I was a high school boy in Southern Ontario. He was a patient in a metropolitan hospital in Toronto. He had entirely lost the power of speech, but he could still write.

He wrote me a few lines in a book on his knee.

I wish I could tell you what he wrote to me that day. His writing was so shaky that I couldn't make out the words. But I could see that it was written in rhymed couplets.

3

Archer in Jeopardy

MOST FICTION IS SHAPED by geography and permeated by autobiography, even when it is trying not to be. Both my father and his father were Scots-Canadian newspaper writers and editors. But I was born about five miles from San Jose, California.

At the dim early edge of memory my parents' marriage broke up, and I became a persistent visitor in the homes of other relatives. The ones I loved most were Aunt Beth and Uncle Rob, with whom I spent two happy years on the shores of Georgian Bay in Ontario.

Rob was an electrician, and held the key to several popular arts. He possessed the only radio in town—he had built it himself—and "Yes-sir, She's My Baby" echoed through my pre-adolescent dreams. On Saturday afternoons it was Rob who opened the movie theater, which had stood dark all week, and admitted any boy or girl who possessed a dime.

For an hour or two, in the flickering semi-darkness, Rob showed us an imaginary world that was realer than the actual one. Chaplin taught us to laugh and cry. Pearl White outwitted the gothic villains who continually threatened her and us. Together they demonstrated that laughter and pain can follow very closely on each other, in a world much like our own but sharper and darker and more brilliant.

Sharper and darker than our world? Perhaps not. Almost before Pearl White had enacted the final escape of her current serial, Aunt Beth died. I was given a train ticket to Winnipeg

15

and placed in a private school by another aunt. There I learned how to grieve for Beth, and for myself, without being noticed by my fellow students or our stoic English masters.

The crash of 1929 propelled me out of Winnipeg and sent me farther west. Before I was out of my teens I had lived with relatives and friends in several dozen houses. I am old enough to be grateful to them now, even to the dangerous one who carried a heavy handgun in his Packard. He may have inspired some of my best work. But I won't name him.

The dead require us to remember and write about them, but I think not to expose them too completely. Though their looming images stay in our minds and become virtually a part of us, they keep their own secrets. Their privacy is necessary to their continuing reality, and to ours. We reinvent them and ourselves out of memory and dreams. And we learn as we grow older to be grateful to the dead. They have cast their flickering shadows across ours, and quicken our reality and their own.

As if they were in adjoining rooms I can hear them talking (not necessarily to each other)—dear Adeline and Uncle Rob who was not my uncle, my two Uncle Edwins who were, my grandmothers and their grandchildren living and dead, my dying father. I can hear them talking in Scots dialect and German and Pennsylvania Dutch and plain English, explaining themselves through six feet of earth impacted over half a century. I hope my books echo (but not too plainly) the feelings which moved my kin when they were alive, the things they were ready to die for, money and music, paintings and each other, fear of God, and their fundamental wish to be remembered, if possible loved.

I love them better now than I did then, and through my stories I understand them better. Sometimes I feel that the stories were written by them to me, asking me to communicate their sorrows and explain their dreams.

My dreams. The underlying theme of many of my novels, as I read them now, is the migration of a mind from one place and culture to another. Its purpose, like the dominant purpose of my young life, was to repossess my American birthplace by imaginative means and heal the schizophrenic pain.

In the end I possess my birthplace and am possessed by its language.

4

Lew Archer,
Private Investigator

IN THE EARLY MONTHS of 1929, when I was thirteen, the most important figure in my imaginative life was Falcon Swift the Monocled Manhunter. Swift was a fictional detective who was regularly featured in the *Boys' Magazine,* a thin pulp magazine with a pink cover which was imported from England and sold for five cents a copy. I bought it every Saturday at a little store on North Main Street in Winnipeg, across the street from the semi-military school where I passed the long Manitoba winter.

The school library was open only on Sunday afternoons. But my nights were enlivened by Falcon Swift's war on evil, his hundred-mile-an-hour journeys by high-powered car across the green face of England, the harsh justice which he meted out to criminals. Reluctant to leave Falcon Swift at Lights Out, I rigged up a mirror which reflected the light from the hallway onto my pillow and enabled me to read, with some difficulty, far into the night.

The stock market crash which took me out of the school in Winnipeg may have saved my eyesight. I never saw another *Boys' Magazine* or heard of Falcon Swift again. But for good or ill he had left his mark on me. Fantastic as his adventures undoubtedly were, they prepared me for (as they derived from) Sherlock Holmes' more cerebral war on evil, Lord Peter Wimsey's towering egotism, and Sapper's low blows. Even when James Bond rose like a Sputnik on the horizon, he seemed not wholly unfamiliar. The Monocled Manhunter was riding again, armed like a battle cruiser, rescuing England from evil domestic and foreign.

A deeper sense of evil (which I associate with Dickens and Wilkie Collins) has come back into the detective form in more recent decades. It reminds us that we live on the slopes of a volcanic history which may erupt again at any time. The evil we are aware of is both public and terribly personal, like an unruly child or an insane relative who has taken up permanent residence in the basement of our lives. At its very best, where it grazes tragedy and transcends its own conventions, detective fiction can remind us that we are all underground men making a brief transit from darkness to darkness.

The typical detective hero in contemporary American fiction speaks for our common humanity. He has an impatience with special privilege, a sense of interdependence among men, and a certain modesty. The central vice of the old-fashioned hero like Holmes or Wimsey, who easily accepted their own superiority, is hubris, an overweening pride and expectation. The central vice of the underground man is moral and social sloth, a willingness to live with whatever is, a molelike inclination to accept the darkness. Perhaps these are the respective vices of aristocracy and democracy.

The private detective is one of the central figures of fiction in which the shift from aristocracy to democracy has visibly occurred, decade by decade. This is true of the real-life detective as well as the fictional, for each imitates the other. The relationship of the imaginary and the actual is further complicated by the fact that fictional detectives tend to be idealized versions of their authors, the kind of men we would choose to be if we were men of action instead of the solitary fantasists we are. Everyone knows this, including the present writer ("I'm not Archer, exactly, but Archer is me.") What everyone may not know is the extent to which actual detectives, both privately and publicly employed, read detective stories and watch crime movies for clues as to how to conduct themselves. One reason why detective fiction is important is that it serves as a model for life and action.

Detectives are human like other men, and the perfect detective will never exist in the flesh. But the several good detectives I have known have certain qualities in common. One is a rather selfless chameleon aspect which allows them to move on various levels of society, ranging from the campus to the slums, and fade in and out of the woodwork on demand. They are able to submerge themselves in the immediate milieu and behave according to its customs and talk the language: a little Spanish in East Los Angeles, a little jive in Watts, a little Levi-Strauss in Westwood. This is something different from the miming of the actor because it is played out in the actual world and is subject to its pressures and uncertainties. The stakes are real.

One night a few years ago I had a phone call from a man who wanted to come out to my house and talk. I remembered his name. A few years before, as a local university student, he had joined the campus branch of the John Birch Society in order to expose its purposes. Since then, he told me in my study, he had carved out a career as a private detective.

Perhaps carved is the wrong word. My visitor was gentle in manner, though he told me he knew karate. Over a period of a year or so, in the Bay area, he had apprehended some fifty criminals. I was surprised by his reason for coming to me. He wanted to establish a code of ethics for private detectives, and thought my Archer stories might serve as a starting point.

Nothing came of that. Events carried him away, as they tend to do with young men of action. I saw him once more, in Superior Court, when he was gathering evidence for the defendants in the Isla Vista trial. Then he went underground on another case, and I haven't seen him since. But let me describe him. He is built like a middleweight, dark and slightly exotic in physical appearance, his dress faintly mod, his hair neither long nor short. His style could be that of a graduate student or an artist, or possibly a young lawyer for the defense. But he is more diffident than self-assertive. He watches and listens, and talks just enough to hold up his end of the conversation. For all his goodwill and energy, there is a touch of sadness in his expression, as if there had been some trouble in his life, a fracture in his world which all his investigative efforts had failed to mend.

I think self-knowledge, and a matching knowledge of the world, are what the serious private detective may be after. I've known a couple of older detectives who had found these things. One of them, an experienced operative from Los Angeles, went into a minority neighborhood where a crime had been committed. Within twenty-four hours, with his white hair and his outgoing democratic manners, he was the friend and virtual confidant of half the families on the block. I know a Nevada detective who works six days a week running down the losers who flock to the gaming tables. On the seventh day he acts as the ombudsman and unofficial justice of the peace for his working-class neighborhood in Reno. He is a good and gentle man, nondescript in appearance, short in height, casual in speech and dress, profoundly offended by violence.

I don't wish to imply that all private detectives scatter kindness. But the ones I've known tend to be reasonable men. If there are sadists and psychopaths among them, they don't last very long in this rather exacting work. The fictional detectives who revel in killing don't belong to the real world. They inhabit a sado-masochistic dream world where no license is required, either for the detective or the wild dreamer at the typewriter.

What makes a private detective, then? Why does he choose the shadow instead of the sunlight? Why does his interest in other men's lives often seem to transcend his interest in his own?

A good private detective has an appetite for life which isn't satisfied by a single role or place. He likes to move through society both horizontally and vertically, studying people like an anthropologist. And like an anthropologist he tends to fall a little in love with his subjects, even if they happen to be the most primitive savages of the urban jungle.

Possibly he became a detective originally in order to make his concern for and knowledge of people possible and then useful. He felt a certain incompleteness in himself which needed to be fulfilled by wide and extraordinary experience. He discovered a certain darkness in himself which could only be explored in terms of badly lighted streets and unknown buildings, alien rooms and the strangers who live in them.

If my detective sounds just a little like a potential criminal or a possible writer, he is meant to. But the criminal seeks out people in order to steal their money or their secrets, or to project himself against them in a rage for power. The detective is tempted by power and knows its uses, but he subordinates a hunger for inordinate power to the requirements of the law and his own desire for understanding and knowledge. The knowl-

20

edge he seeks is ultimately self-knowledge, and like his sedentary brother the writer he finds himself in the course of his life if he's lucky.

The detective who is at the center of my early stories, particularly the very early ones, is not the Lew Archer of the later novels. In the original version of the first story, "Find the Woman," the detective was a young man who called himself Evans, I believe. Nor was "The Bearded Lady" originally an Archer story. In its first version it was about a young naval officer (which I had recently been) and was written as a novelette for *The American Magazine.* I wrote some stories for *Manhunt* and *Ellery Queen's Mystery Magazine,* which fortunately continues to sustain mystery writers between the novelist's widely separated paydays. "Midnight Blue" was written for *Ed McBain's Mystery Magazine,* and "The Sleeping Dog" was commissioned by *Sports Illustrated* but ultimately published by *Argosy.*

The writing of these stories was scattered over two decades or more, and naturally they vary in style and interest. The early ones particularly show my debt to other writers, especially Hammett and Chandler, and in fact did not aim at any striking originality. They helped to support and instruct me while I learned my trade and began to learn my art.

It could be said that the early stories are the price I paid to become a professional writer. Short and few as they are, the writing of them altered me. I accepted a limitation of form and style which opened up a world but changed me, or a part of me, from Kenneth Millar into Ross Macdonald.

As a man writes his fiction, his fiction is writing him. We can never change ourselves back into what we were, any more than I can change these printed words. So we have to be careful about what we write.

5

Kenneth Millar/
Ross MacDonald
—A Checklist

Having a bibliography put together is in some ways like being psychoanalyzed. Forgotten days of your life are rediscovered. But where the effect of a successful analysis is to revalue and in a sense revoke the past, a successful bibliography puts it permanently into the record. A psychoanalyst may hazard an educated guess that once upon a time his subject entertained a certain fantasy; the bibliographer is in a position to prove it.

To be confronted all at once with the record of nearly everything that one has ever written can be a sobering experience. A bibliography is to an old writer what a rap sheet is to a three-time loser.

Is it possible that this man can be rehabilitated? the internal prosecutor says to the imaginary judge. Just look at his record, your honor. He committed his first public crime when he was fifteen, and he has been helplessly repeating it for nearly forty years. The only way to protect society from this incorrigible malefactor is to lock him up and throw away the key.

One is moved to explanation and apology. I was born with a fatal predisposition to words. Both my father and my grandfather were journalists, and there were writers on my mother's side of the family. My Uncle Rob, with whom I lived for a while after my parents were separated, used to tell me animal stories every weekday, and on Saturdays he took me to the movies to see such serials as Pearl White's "Plunder." The terrors with which the episodes ended, the satisfactions with which they

23

began, left a permanent impression on my nerves. My own life, as I moved from home to home and relative to relative, seemed as episodic and unpredictable as a movie serial, or the *Black Mask* fiction I read in my teens.

I began to write verse and fiction before I reached my teens. When I was twelve, resident in a boys' school in Winnipeg, I filled the empty hours when the gym was closed writing a sheaf of western stories and a long narrative poem about Bonnie Prince Charlie. I think I was searching for a tradition that would relate to my life and the place. My grandfather came from Scotland; Prince Charlie and the Stuarts were its lost kings. The Canadian west, a remote province of Great Britain which is only now being staked out by native imaginations, seemed infinitely cold and empty in those winters.

The crash of 1929 propelled me out of the school in Winnipeg, where my father's sister had been paying my tuition. After a year with my mother's sister, Laura, in Medicine Hat, Alberta, I went back to the family's original home in Ontario, and lived with my mother in her mother's house until I finished high school. The year I graduated, 1932, I counted the rooms I had lived in during my first sixteen years, and got a total of fifty. Novelists are made, if they are made at all, out of uncertain beginnings and long delayed completions, like their books.

Canada was alive with lyric poets at that time, but had few novelists. Its dominant prose writer was Stephen Leacock, acknowledged as the founder of modern North American humor by Robert Benchley and Scott Fitzgerald. I was reading Dashiell Hammett and Dostoevsky, but my first published story was a parody of Conan Doyle written under the obvious influence of Leacock.

My wife Margaret Millar keeps in a special box a copy of the Kitchener Collegiate Institute *Grumbler* in which this first story appeared. Her own first story, about a dying pianist in Spain, is in it, too. Elsewhere in that old school magazine, dogeared after nearly forty years, we can find more direct images of our adolescent lives. Margaret and I are there with the other members of the high school debating team, gazing confidently out of the picture on the page into eight more years of depression and six of war.

About six years later, in another city, I walked into the public library and found Margaret reading Thucydides in Greek. From then on, we saw each other nearly every day. I was just back from Europe, determined to become a writer. Margaret confessed she had the same ambition. We were married in June, 1938, the day after I graduated from college, and honeymooned at summer school in Ann Arbor. In the fall we went on to the University of Toronto, where I prepared to become a high school teacher.

The following spring I became at the same time the father of a daughter and a professional writing for money. My main market was the Toronto political and literary weekly, *Saturday Night*. I lightly bombarded the editor, B. K. Sandwell, with verses and humorous sketches, and my first few realistic stories. *Saturday Night* came out on Saturday morning, and we used to walk up Bloor Street to see if anything of mine had been printed that week. Payment was just a cent a word, but the early joys of authorship were almost as sweet as sex. I felt as if Toronto, that unknown city of stone, had opened an eye and looked at me, then relapsed into her dream of commerce.

We had a very Canadian eagerness to make something of ourselves. While I taught in our old high school in the winter, and studied at Ann Arbor in the summer, Margaret began to write mystery novels. Her books were humorous at first, then veered through the Gothic mode toward tragedy. Their success enabled me to leave high school teaching after two years and accept a full-time fellowship at the University of Michigan. Margaret's work was enabling to me in another way. By going on ahead and breaking trail, she helped to make it possible for me to become a novelist, as perhaps her life with me had helped to make it possible for her.

My first novel was written in Ann Arbor in the fall of 1943. I worked on it at night in one of the offices of the main classroom building, and the book preserves some of the atmosphere of that empty echoing pile. Part of the terror that permeates the book was my own terror, I think, at the act of committing myself to a long piece of writing. It also reflects less immediate experiences. In the winter of 1936-37 I had dropped out of school and gone to Europe, where I spent two months in Nazi Germany. More recently, I had been turned down on physical

25

grounds for a commission in the United States Naval Reserve. Later the Navy relaxed its standards and by the time *The Dark Tunnel* was published, I was in Officers Candidate School at Princeton. My second book was written a year or so later aboard an escort carrier in the Pacific. Then I came home to California, where Margaret and our daughter now lived, and between March 1946 and the end of that year, in a kind of angry rapture, wrote *Blue City* and *The Three Roads*.

The first was about the underlife of an imaginary American city, abstracted from the several cities the war had taken me to. *The Three Roads* was my first California novel, written when I had spent no more than a few days on leave in Los Angeles. But I had met writers there—Joe Pagano, Elliot Paul, John Collier—and they gave me the feel of that extraordinary city. It seemed like the capital of an unknown civilization, barely remembered, or dimly foreseen.

One of the two main characters in *The Three Roads*, Paula West, begins a railroad journey from San Diego to Los Angeles as follows:

> The shining metal streamliner standing beside the station added the final touch to her allegory. It was the impossible future superimposed upon the ugly present in the presence of the regretted past. There was no continuity between the tenses, she thought. You passed from one to the other as a ghost passed through a wall, at the risk of your own reality. The spotless interior of this streamlined future was crowded with unreal passengers waiting to be transported, appropriately enough, to Los Angeles.

Such a moderately ambitious passage as this brings up the question of why I chose to write crime fiction instead of straight fiction. I had less choice than the reader may suppose. My one attempt to write a regular autobiographical novel about my unhappy childhood turned out so badly that I never showed it to my publisher. I left the manuscript, I think, in an abandoned blacking factory. The deadly game of social Snakes and Ladders which occupied much of my youth had to be dealt with in another form, more impersonal and objective.

26

I had other reasons for writing detective stories. The work of Hammett and Chandler and their fellow-writers seemed to constitute a popular and democratic literature such as Frank Norris had called for in "The Responsibilities of the Novelist." Their heroes seemed to continue in highly complicated urban environments the masculine and egalitarian frontier traditions of Natty Bumppo and his nineteenth-century descendants. Their abrupt and striking scenes seemed to reflect the disjunctions of an atomized society. Their style, terse and highly figured, seemed not quite to have reached the end of its development.

Certainly the world they wrote about had not. The rush of change which the war had started continued and accelerated afterwards, particularly in the empty spaces of California. It seemed that a brave new world was being born here, on the last frontier, and people migrated to it as we had from all over the continent. I wrote about the far side of the brave new world, in a series of hardboiled detective stories which began in 1949 with *The Moving Target.*

"Hardboiled" is rather a misnomer for this kind of story. Its distinctive ingredient is a style which tries to catch the rhythms and some of the words of the spoken language. While the essential features of its plot are a crime and a solution, there is room in the form for complexities of meaning which can match those of the traditonal novel. It is a form which lends itself to the depiction, at the same time energetic and disenchanted, of the open society which California in the years just after the war was struggling to become.

I needed time, and deeper personal knowledge of that society, before I could make it entirely my own in fiction, or make the California detective novel my own. Raymond Chandler was and remains a hard man to follow. He wrote like a slumming angel, and invested the sun-blinded streets of Los Angeles with a romantic presence. While trying to preserve the fantastic lights and shadows of the actual Los Angeles, I gradually siphoned off the aura of romance and made room for a completer social realism. My detective Archer is not so much a knight of romance as an observer, a socially mobile man who knows all the levels of Southern California life and takes a peculiar wry pleasure in exploring its secret passages. Archer tends to live through other people, as a novelist lives through his characters.

In the course of the first three Archer novels, I tried to work out my own version of the "hardboiled" style, to develop both imagery and structure in the direction of psychological and symbolic meaning. In the fourth, *The Ivory Grin* (1952), I extended the range of the form beyond California, touching on Boston and Montreal, Chicago and Detroit; and doing a portrait of a gangster family which was unblurred by any romantic admiration. But it took me five more novels, and seven more years, to work out within the limits of this rather difficult craft the kind of story that I was aiming at: a story roughly shaped on my own early life, transformed and simplified into a kind of legend, in *The Galton Case*.

Even here I approached my life from a distance, and crept up on it in disguise as one might track an alien enemy; the details of the book were all invented. But there was personal truth in its broad shape, as I have explained elsewhere. In crossing the border from Canada and making my way in stages to my birthplace in California, I had learned the significance of borders. They make the difference between legitimacy and fraudulence, and we cross them 'as a ghost passes through a wall, at the risk of our own reality.'

Perhaps *The Galton Case* validated my journey, and made it possible for my mind to look both north to Canada and south to Mexico and Panama, in later books like *The Zebra-Striped Hearse* and *Black Money*. At any rate it thawed my autobiographical embarrassment and started a run of somewhat more personal fiction which has, for better or worse, gone on unabated ever since. Of my twenty-three books, the three I have just named are among my favorites. They have a certain intensity and range.

But one writes on a curve, on the backs of torn-off calendar sheets. A writer in his fifties will not recapture the blaze of youth, or the steadier passion that comes like a second and saner youth in his forties, if he's lucky. But he can lie in wait in his room—it must be at least the hundredth room by now—and keep open his imagination and the bowels of his compassion against the day when another book will haunt him like a ghost rising out of both the past and the future.

6

Archer at Large

PEOPLE OFTEN ASK me when and how I became a professional writer. I think I can say when. How, and possibly why, may emerge in the telling.

In early June of 1939, in Toronto, I was a student teacher with no money and a very pregnant wife. I left Margaret at home one afternoon in order to hear Lord Tweedsmuir deliver a high school graduation address. Lord Tweedsmuir was the Governor-General of Canada at that time, but the reason I went to hear him was that he was also John Buchan, the author of *The Thirty-Nine Steps.*

He turned out to be a small, bright-eyed Scot who wore the mantle of empire easily. At the climax of his speech he told the graduating seniors the old story of the race between the hare and the tortoise. But he told it with a difference. The hare fooled around a good deal while the slow dependable tortoise stuck to the course and never even looked up. Still the hare won easily. Lord Tweedsmuir drew the moral that the race is not always to the slow.

About this time I won a typewriter on a radio quiz show and started immediately to write for publication. I like to think that the Governor-General inspired me; but like most other would-be writers I drew on more mundane sources of inspiration. Though I had a teaching job waiting in the fall at my old high school in Kitchener, Margaret and I had nothing to live on between June and September. My wife's approaching

29

confinement and the prospective hospital bill made the situation urgent.

If I had been a genuine hare, I'd have dashed off a detective novel in about three weeks, sent it to the biggest publisher in New York, and got an immediate acceptance by telegram. (A year or so later Margaret did just that.) I aimed lower, at tortoise level, writing a flock of short stories and sketches for quickly available Toronto markets, most of which were so-called Sunday School papers paying a cent a word. I made over a hundred dollars the first few weeks, and with this blessed wad of cash ransomed my wife and infant daughter out of the Women's College Hospital. I was a pro.

Our lives changed rapidly in the next five years. Margaret became a full-fledged novelist. I left high school teaching to accept a fellowship at the University of Michigan, and moved my family to the United States, where I was born. In June 1944, when my first novel was published (*The Dark Tunnel*, a novel of espionage suggested by my own experiences in Nazi Germany but showing the influence of John Buchan) I was an ensign in the U.S. Naval Reserve. When I was released from service, as I recorded in the introduction to *Archer in Hollywood*, I settled down in my native state, in Santa Barbara, and became a California crime novelist.

Ten years and ten novels later, seismic disturbances occurred in my life. My half-suppressed Canadian years, my whole childhood and youth, rose like a corpse from the bottom of the sea to confront me. Margaret and I moved to the Bay area for a year, settling not many miles from my birthplace in Los Gatos. There I went through belated mental growing pains, trying to understand the peculiar shape of my life.

The inner shape of a man's life, if he is a man of action, plots the curve of his movements. If he is a writer, it is what he writes from and about. But it remains as personal and hidden as his skeleton, just as intricate, almost as unchangeable.

Since I couldn't change the shape of my life, I decided to make the best of it. In the summer of 1957 Margaret and I returned to Santa Barbara and rented a house on a cliff which overlooked the sea. A further advantage of the neighborhood was that the English poet Donald Davie was living nearby. We became friends, and I learned that Davie was working on the epic theme of a lost father. After my year's immersion in memories of my own past, a similar theme was growing in my mind.

The theme developed through the fall and winter. (It's fall on the California coast when migrating sea birds move in dark skeins across the blue water; we call it winter when it rains a bit.) As I sat in my study looking out over the sea, I was conscious that a few hundred yards away along the cliff, Davie was writing his epic poem. His working presence nerved me to commit a legend of my own to paper, and I wrote what I considered a breakthrough novel, *The Galton Case*.

What did it break through into? My early years in Canada, for one thing. I hardly knew my father. My mother and I lived, when we were lucky, on the charity of her mother and her sister. They were good women (Aunt Adeline, who paid for my education, was a Stoic saint) but in their puritanical household I felt both surrounded and displaced. I was my wandering father's son, after all, and my mother's female relatives could hardly help discerning on my brow the mark of the paternal curse.

One of the things that supported me through my long Canadian childhood was the knowledge, which my mother insisted on, that I was an American citizen by birth. But for good or ill my early days made a Canadian out of me as well. I ended up split along emotional and political lines which neatly corresponded. My sense of self and my sense of territory were both askew.

The Galton Case goes into some of these matters. It doesn't tell the naked truth, of course. It broke free of my actual life and my rather murky feelings, into the clearer and more ordered world where fiction lays out its concentrated, terrifying versions of the truth. Fiction, when it is working well, lifts out of the writer's life patterns which tend toward the legendary. But the patterns are disrupted and authenticated by bits and pieces of the original life-stuff—names and places, scraps of conversation, old feelings and forces like spawning salmon working their way back up the stream of time.

A central figure in *The Galton Case* is a nameless boy who has taken the name of John (my father's name). When this fictional John made his way to Ann Arbor and entered the

31

University of Michigan, he was following in my footsteps. John and I had other things in common. We shared a sense of displacement, a feeling that, no matter where we were, we were on the alien side of some border. We felt like dubious claimants to a lost inheritance.

Still, any novel worth writing has a strong positive aspect, conforming to and filling out the shape of the novelist's life. Writing is an action as well as a passion. In writing *The Galton Case* and mastering its materials, I felt an exhilaration which I hope the book communicates to its readers. For me, in its indirect way, it stated and made good the right to my inheritance as an American citizen and writer, while bringing into unsparing view the poverty and brokenness of my worst days.

7

Find the Woman

FIND THE WOMAN was written underwater, somewhere between San Francisco and Kwajalein, in the early fall of 1945. I was a Communications Officer aboard the U.S.S. *Shipley Bay*, an escort carrier, and my cabin was below the waterline, in that charming situation known as Torpedo Junction. The Japanese war was over, the ship had been converted into a troop transport, and there were no more sixteen-hour days in the coding room. The first night out, I pulled the opening chapters of a novel out of a box. I had written them the previous year, after my first book was published. They failed to excite me. Perhaps I needed some kind of warmup before going on with the novel. The night before, over drinks in a San Francisco hotel room, Tony Boucher had told me about Ellery Queen's first annual short story contest and suggested I enter a story in it. I started to think about plots.

My wife Margaret was working for Warner Brothers that year, writing a screenplay for "The Iron Gates." A few weeks before, I had spent a ten-day leave with her in Hollywood. (Transport duty on the pineapple run was good duty.) The contrast between the comparative simplicity of life at sea and the complexity of human relations on shore must have struck me forcibly. Anyway, it gave me the outlines of a plot. The final twist in the plot occurred to me as I wrote. With Boucher's encouragement and a year's accumulation of frustration behind my pen, the story wrote itself in two evenings. Three weeks later, when the *Shipley Bay* wallowed into port again, the novel was finished, too. Those were the days.

The original title of the story was "Death by Water." Ellery Queen gave it a better title and a four hundred dollar prize. I still like it pretty well, in spite of its obvious stylistic debt to Raymond Chandler. I suppose you could describe it as Chandler with onions. But then Chandler himself is Hammett with Freud potatoes. As Dostoevsky said about Gogol (I think), we all came out from under Hammett's black mask.

8

Archer in Hollywood

THE WAR had a great deal to do with my becoming a professional writer. It plucked me out of graduate school, gave me a rough, short course in American geography and society, and sent me back to my native California. It provided me with the subject matter for my first two books, which were spy novels. In a way it gave me matter for all my books. Crime, as *The Moving Target* seems to imply, is often war continued by other means.

My Navy discharge papers (March, 1946) said hopefully that my first choice for civilian employment was "freelance writer in California." We lived that year in a four-room stucco house on Bath Street in Santa Barbara. It had orange trees in the back yard but no central heating. My wife and I used to sit and write in our overcoats. It was a lucky, slightly chilly year and by the end of it I had written two books, *Blue City* and *The Three Roads*, which Alfred Knopf liked well enough to publish.

The next year wasn't so lucky. I felt it was now my duty to write an autobiographical novel about my depressing childhood in Canada. I tried, and got badly bogged down in sloppy feelings and groping prose. I began to doubt my vocation as a writer and my mind turned back toward the comparative safety of graduate school.

I was in trouble, and Lew Archer got me out of it. I resembled one of his clients in needing a character to front for me. Like many other writers—the most extreme example is a man I knew who wrote fiction from the point of view of his pet turtle—I couldn't work directly with my own experiences and feelings. A narrator had to be interposed, like protective lead, between me and the radioactive material.

Raymond Chandler had recently shown, in a brilliant series of novels, how a private detective could be used to block off overpersonal excitements while getting on with the story. Archer in his early days, though he was named for Sam Spade's partner, was patterned on Chandler's Marlowe. Chandler's Anglo-American background and my Canadian-American one gave our detectives a common quality: the fresh suspicious eye of a semi-outsider who is fascinated but not completely taken in by the customs of the natives.

We shared, for related reasons, a powerful interest in the American colloquial language. Democracy is as much a language as it is a place. If a man has suffered (as we both had) under a society of privilege, the American vernacular can serve him as a kind of passport to freedom and equality. Marlowe and Archer can go anywhere, at least once, and talk to anybody. Their rough-and-ready brand of democracy is still peculiarly rampant on this side of the Sierra Nevada.

If California is a state of mind, Hollywood is where you take its temperature. There is a peculiar sense in which this city existing mainly on film and tape is our national capital, alas, and not just the capital of California. It's the place where our children learn how and what to dream and where everything happens just before, or just after, it happens to us.

American novelists have a lover's quarrel with Hollywood. We have grown accustomed to losing it. Our finest novelist Scott Fitzgerald felt in his uncertain last years that the art of film was the master art that had superseded the novel. The hero of his last, unfinished novel was a movie producer.

My lover's quarrel with Hollywood began at the age of seven when, on successive Saturday afternoons in my uncle's theater, I formed a precocious attachment to Pearl White. The quarrel and the attachment have since taken more devious forms. One thing that strikes me, over and above a recurrent fascination with Hollywood, is my use of film techniques. *The Moving Target* in particular is a story clearly aspiring to be a movie. It was no accident that when Warner Brothers made it into one

36

last year they were able to follow the story virtually scene by scene.

I remember how I labored over those scenes, striking them out in heat and then reworking them over and over for more than a year. I was no longer writing at home. My sister-in-law Dorothy Schlagel had an apartment nearby on Sola Street. It was vacant all day while Dorothy was at work, and I wrote there.

By 1950, when I wrote *The Way Some People Die*, Dorothy had moved to a house on the far side of town and I rode over every morning on a motor scooter. The labor I'd put into forming a style in *Target* had begun to pay off. Rummaging through old papers the other day, I found the opening paragraph of *Way* written out in a spiral notebook, for the first and final time, just as it was to be printed.

Some of my colleagues—Mike Avallone is one—think that *Way* is the best of my twenty books. I hope it isn't. If it were it would mean I'd been over the hill for sixteen or seventeen years, which is the unthinkable dread of every writer past the age of forty.

The Barbarous Coast was written when I was forty. Though I've always been a slow developer, by that time I was getting myself and my form under more personal control. It was my largest book so far, in both social range and moral complexity. In it I was learning to get rid of the protective wall between my mind and the perilous stuff of my own life.

I'm not and never was George Wall, the angry young Canadian lost in Hollywood. But I once lived, as George did, on Spadina Avenue in Toronto. Like the three young divers in the story, I was a tower diver before my bones got brittle. And I once went to a party not wholly unlike the long party in the book.

We writers, as we work our way deeper into our craft, learn to drop more and more personal clues. Like burglars who secretly wish to be caught, we leave our fingerprints on the broken locks, our voiceprints in the bugged rooms, our footprints in the wet concrete and the blowing sand.

9

In The First Person

(from the Davidson Films shooting script)

I TOOK THE NAME "Ross Macdonald" because Macdonald was a family name. My father's name was John Macdonald Millar—I don't know where the "Ross" came from. It's a Scottish name and I come from Scottish people on my father's side. Innumerable traces of my life run through my books. Most of them have to do with a broken family and a lost father. My father was the son of a first-generation Scots newspaper editor in Ontario. When he was still in his teens, he went west to Alberta and British Columbia. He supported himself as a journalist, but he was essentially a poet and a writer. My mother, too, was a Canadian and a British subject.

I was born in Los Gatos, California, during the first World War. My parents moved to Vancouver, where my father became a harbor pilot. He was a good friend of the Japanese fishermen who used the harbor, and some of my earliest playmates were Japanese children. Like my father, I have always been fascinated by the ocean. My mother started to take me bathing when I was two or three. I still swim in the ocean nearly every day, and I get some of my best ideas in the water.

One of my father's best friends was an old prospector and trapper name Joe Brewer. He had suffered from snow blindness in the Yukon Gold Rush and lost his sight. Joe Brewer gave me a hunting knife which I treasured all through my boyhood—proof and symbol of my contact with the frontier.

My early life in Vancouver was a good background for a

novelist; I got to know so many different kinds of people and heard so many voices. We hardly realize the impress of experience and memory laid down in a child's mind. Some of the things that make a man into an artist or a writer are the events that happen before we are supposed to understand them, when we are actually laying down the foundations of our own version of the world.

My parents' marriage broke up when we were living in Vancouver. My mother took me on the transcontinental train across the Rocky Mountains and the prairies to her old home in Ontario. Before I was sixteen I lived in fifty different rooms— rented rooms in rooming houses or in the homes of relatives— and all over the Canadian west and Southern Ontario.

When I was six, my mother, without resources, prepared to place me in an orphanage. But a cousin of my father, Rob Millar, took me into his home. Later, when I was ready to start high school my father's sister, my Aunt Margaret, sent me to St. John's School in Winnipeg. This school gave me an insight into how the more prosperous families lived; through my boyhood I was given a very thorough grounding in various levels of society. That is one of the things I write about now, the relationship between the various parts of society.

I finished my high school days in my grandmother's home in Kitchener, Ontario. I was an unwanted guest in the house, and it gradually became a place I only visited when I wanted to sleep. My second home was the public library.

At this time my father was felled by a series of strokes, and came home to Ontario to die. My mother, who was a nurse, helped him in his worst periods in the hospital. He was still writing poetry when I went to see him in the last year of his life—even though he could no longer speak.

I think my father's example, combined with the lack of any other outlet, made a writer of me.

I began to write verse and fiction before I was twelve. Poe's tales made a great impression on me. Also, I was reading Dickens' *Oliver Twist.* Dickens would never have become the novelist he was if he hadn't had a troubled childhood. I began to have the dream of being a professional, like Dickens, who wrote for the popular market and at the same time expressed his deepest feelings.

40

When I was younger I used to read *Huckleberry Finn* at least once a year. It is a wonderful example of an artist using the actual spoken language. For years I was planning my own raft trip down the Mississippi. Huck Finn was not Mark Twain, but Mark Twain used him to express his own ideas about a slave-owning society. The book I read nearly every year now is *The Great Gatsby* by F. Scott Fitzgerald. Like Stephen Crane and Mark Twain, Fitzgerald listened to people talking before he sat down to write. Good writers not only learn from people talking, they teach other people how to talk. And how to write.

During the twenties and thirties I lived in various cities large and small, and saw a good deal of gambling and corruption. But I didn't get a picture of the way cities were run until I found the novels of Dashiell Hammett. They did a great deal to turn me in the direction of the hard-boiled mystery novel. The term hard-boiled is not necessarily connected with violence, it has more to do with a realistic attitude toward life as reflected in the language.

Hammett and Stephen Crane taught me the modern American style based on the speaking voice. Most modern prose is based on the spoken language. A writer has to learn to listen to the sound of his own and other people's voices. Crane formed his style to a great extent by listening. When he was writing *The Red Badge of Courage,* a novel about the Civil War, he listened to Civil War veterans talk. These books represent an oral tradition, they are derived from the spoken language which is actually the carrier of our social and cultural meanings. It's what people say to each other, in their own tone of voice, that really counts in life. If you get such a tone of voice and a sense of actual speech in your writing, you have something better than literary prose. There is more to it than that, of course. The dream of the whole North American experience is to build, on new territory, a democratic society where there will be one language spoken by all men. I hope the dream won't be lost.

Such a dream requires a language in print similar to the way men talk. People should read a book and recognize themselves talking. In order to have a democratic society, you have to have a classless language. In order to maintain the language, the highest product of any civilization, you have to write fiction in the spoken language. This is the whole idea of the democratic novel which Frank Norris, another of my masters, wrote about in his "Responsibilities of the Novelist."

Apart from a few blazing geniuses, most beginning writers inevitably imitate the writers they admire. Of course, they admire those writers because they are doing things they would like to be able to do. They learn those techniques of writing by seeing how other writers do them. A writer with any real stuff will learn from a number of different writers.

My first published story appeared in a high school magazine in 1931. It was a burlesque of Sherlock Holmes written under the influence of the Canadian humorist Stephen Leacock. My wife Margaret Millar keeps in a special box a copy of the Kitchener Collegiate Institute *Grumbler* in which this first story appeared. Her own first story, about a dying pianist in Spain, is in it, too. Elsewhere in that old school magazine, dog-eared after nearly forty years, we can find more direct images of our teen-age lives. Margaret and I are there with the other members of the high school debating team, gazing confidently out of the picture into eight more years of depression and six of war.

About six years later, in another city, I walked into the public library and found Margaret reading Thucydides in Greek. From then on, we saw each other nearly every day. I was just back from Europe, determined to become a writer. Margaret confessed she had the same ambition. The day after I graduated from college Margaret and I were married. We had a very Canadian eagerness to make something of ourselves. I taught at our old high school in the winter, studied at Ann Arbor in the summer, and began to write professionally on the side. At the same time, Margaret began to write mystery novels. Her books were humorous at first, then moved into psychological horror and suspense. Her first novel, *Beast In View*, was given the Edgar Allen Poe award as best mystery novel of the year. Reading and helping on my wife's work, several of which were written before any of my books, had a great influence on my own work. I learned how to construct a mystery in the process of working with Margaret, but I wrote my own books in the American hard-boiled style. The leading American hard-boiled novelists, James M. Cain, Dashiell Hammett, and Raymond Chandler, had all been published by Alfred Knopf. When he

42

became my publisher in 1949, I felt as if I had joined a select company of writers, presided over by the leading literary publisher in America.

I have often thought there are no false starts in preparing to write a novel. However, you get many ideas you aren't able to use, or aren't ready to use. I generally write about three different plots and develop them side by side to see which one I am ready to do. But then when I write the novel I sometimes use all three of them. The one novel absorbs all the material. As you get older you get harder to please, you are no longer satisfied with your first idea, either for a sentence or a book. Sometimes, I've spent just about as long planning a book and deciding exactly how I'm going to start it and write it as I do writing the actual book. I might spend four or five months planning a book when I put all the time together. Then, when I am ready to do it, I write it almost without stopping. That doesn't mean I hurry. The actual writing is the real work. Anybody can make notes for unwritten novels, and a lot of people have. The real work is to write it. After I served my apprenticeship to Hammett and Raymond Chandler, I had to learn to write my own kind of novel. It was not about professional criminals, but about the lives of middle class people whose crises erupt in crime. I learned in attending trials that the average murderer is not a professional, nor even necessarily a person who has committed other crimes. Typically he explodes under the pressures of his own life. His victim is often a friend or a member of his family. These are the kinds of human situations I tried to realize in my fiction.

The basic idea of a detective story is to create a puzzle and provide a solution. But I also want to give the reader a full novel at the same time. I am not content unless I am giving myself and the reader everything in my capabilities, this is something an artist wants—to give everything he has to the work at hand. A detective novelist, like any other novelist, is trying to give a true sense of human life as he sees it.

I don't always use my latest ideas right away. I try to write from my oldest ideas and memories. The longer a book is allowed to grow in the mind, the more likely it is to absorb the full meaning of one's life and to take the particular curve and bend of the writer's mind. What we are all really trying to do is leave a record of ourselves just as we are, different from everybody else, like fingerprints.

The longest I have held a book in my mind before I wrote it is about twenty years. I think I had the central idea for *Black Money* in my mind for close to twenty years. It took me all that time to figure out how I could write it and to decide where the central character came from, who he was and what the source of the black money was. Year after year I would return to these ideas, make more notes and a cross reference to a twenty-year-old notebook and put it away until I was ready to work on it.

I always start with an idea, and the idea usually contains in it the possibility of a strong reversal so that one thing appears to be the case, and then it turns out to be something quite radically different. In *Black Money*, for example, Francis Martel appears as a major threat at first, but in the end turns out to be a victim. Generally I start out with a kernel of an idea for a plot with a series of events, or a main event, that appears to explain itself in a certain way. As the book progresses, I weigh into the story other events which may turn it in an entirely different direction.

All mystery novels by definition have to be constructed in terms of puzzle and solution. What I try to do is make both the initial statements valid and interesting and the solution even more valid and interesting. In other words, the solution fills out the meaning of what has gone before. The reversal is actually an illumination of what has gone before.

There are two absolute strict requirements in writing a mystery, one is to keep the reader interested in your story and your characters, the other is to keep concealed from him what is actually happening. I sacrifice, if sacrifice is the word, everything to those two requirements. Fiction is a human art like architecture, providing mental space for people to live in. A novel is trying to give a picture of life as it is lived over a period of time and a span of space, it is a complex structure, more complex than a house. A writer has to plan a book before he starts to build it, otherwise he is going to find himself building in the wrong place and putting in the wrong shapes.

Francis Martel, in *Black Money*, like John Brown in *The Galton Case*, was suggested by my own experiences. Both Francis and John crossed a border, as I had, into the United

44

States, and attempted to start radically new lives in California. During this entire period, California has been the magnet among the states, drawing people from all over the continent, from all over the world. California was movieland, where anything could happen.

Like most children of my time, I was deeply influenced by the movies. Rob Millar, with whom I spent some happy early years, ran the movie theatre in Wiarton, Ontario. I saw some thrilling serials, including "Robinson Crusoe" and Pearl White's cliff-hanger "Plunder." I waited in suspense from week to week for the next episode. These experiences probably had a great deal to do with the cinematic elements of my style. There is a scene in *The Instant Enemy*, for example, which could have been the climax of an episode in any cliff-hanger. But there are old American traditions affecting my hero, too—the tradition of James Fenimore Cooper's frontiersman, Natty Bumppo, known as "Hawkeye," merging with the tradition of Joe Brewer who gave me my first knife.

I don't spend much time describing a scene. It's better not to put in too many details; let the reader imagine the scene, give him some guidelines and let him go from there. The opening of my novel *The Instant Enemy* illustrates what I mean:

"There was light early morning traffic on Sepulveda. As I drove over the low pass, the sun came up glaring behind the blue crags on the far side of the valley. For a minute or two, before regular day set in, everything looked fresh and new and awesome as creation."

There is very little detail here, but what there is is accurate and points to a definite time and place. We've started out with Archer driving over to the San Fernando Valley and end up comparing it to the First Day.

A novelist has the ability to go back, clear to the very beginnings of his life, his troubles, his sorrows and convert them into something that will be pleasing and satisfying to him, and meaningful to other people. I can take a three-year-old's loss of his father, which was nothing but an undiluted sorrow at the time, and make a whole book out of it. Thousands of people will read and understand and use it to explain, in an imaginative sense, some of their own trouble. We all suffer terrible losses, we all go through the troubles of life. The purpose of art is to put them in a context so we can see not just the troubles but the meaning of them, where they came from and where they lead. It isn't sorrow and trouble we can't stand, but meaningless sorrow, trouble that leads nowhere. A novel helps us all, including the writer himself, make sense of our lives.

I don't write from life, I don't write about an actual person that I've ever known or seen. When I write about somebody like Francis Martel in *Black Money*, a Panamanian boy who would seem at first glance to have nothing to do with me, I'm not just drawing on my memories of Panama, I'm actually writing out of the shape of my own life.

The writer lives life more fully, more intensely and more sensitively than other people. But he does it through a screen or a glass and as you become older in writing, you find the best things and the worst things that happen to you are on paper. I suppose that is what art is all about. It's a transfer of life, from living and breathing, to some other medium where it can be seen more steadily, and at the same time with feeling but without the intense pain, without the numbing, blinding, and terrifying pain that life gives you. It enables you and your readers to pass through experiences which you could hardly survive in life, but which in fiction can leave you not only unhurt, but even enhanced with more understanding of what life is.

10

Writing The Galton Case

D ETECTIVE STORY WRITERS are often asked why we devote
our talents to working in a mere popular convention. One
answer is that there may be more to our use of the convention
than meets the eye. I tried to show in an earlier piece how the
literary detective has provided writers since Poe with a disguise, a kind of welder's mask enabling us to handle dangerously hot material.

One night in his fifth year when we were alone in my house,
my grandson Jimmie staged a performance which demonstrated the uses of disguise. His main idea seemed to be to
express and discharge his guilts and fears, particularly his
overriding fear that his absent parents might punish his (im-
perceptible) moral imperfections by never coming back
to him. Perhaps he had overheard and been alarmed by the
name of the movie they were attending, *Divorce American
Style.*

Jimmie's stage was the raised hearth in the kitchen, his only
prop a towel. He climbed up on the hearth and hid himself
behind the back of an armchair. "Grandpa, what do you see?"

"Nothing."

He put the towel in view. "What do you see now?"

"Your towel."

He withdrew the towel. There was a silence. "What am I
doing with my towel?"

I guessed that he was doing something "wrong," and that

he wanted me to suspend judgment. "You're chewing it," I said boldly.

"No. But I have it in my mouth."

My easy acceptance of his wickedness encouraged him to enact it before my eyes. His head popped up. He was completely hooded with the towel, like a miniature inductee into the Ku Klux Klan.

"I'm a monster," he announced.

Then he threw off the towel, laughing. I sat and watched him for a time while the hooded monster and the laughing boy took alternate possession of the stage. Finally, soothed and purged by his simple but powerful art, Jimmie lay down on the cushioned hearth and went to sleep.

His little show speaks for itself, and needs no Aristotle. But let me point out some connections between his monodrama and my detective fiction. Both draw directly on life and feed back into it. Both are something the artist does for his own sake. But they need an audience to fulfill even their private function, let alone their public ones. Disguise is the imaginative device which permits the work to be both private and public, to half-divulge the writer's crucial secrets while deepening the whole community's sense of its own mysterious life.

I was forty-two when I wrote *The Galton Case*. It had taken me a dozen years and as many books to learn to tell highly personal stories in terms of the convention I had chosen. In the winter of 1957-1958 I was as ready as I would ever be to cope in fiction with some of the more complicated facts of my experience.

Central among these was the fact that I was born in California, in 1915, and was thus an American citizen; but I was raised in Canada by Canadian relatives. After attending university in Canada, I taught high school there for two years. In 1941, in one of the decisive moves of my life, I came back to the United States with my wife and young daughter, and started work on a doctorate in English at the University of Michigan.

It was a legitimate move, but the crossing of the border failed to dispel my dual citizen's sense of illegitimacy, and probably deepened it. This feeling was somewhat relieved by a couple of years in the American Navy. After the war I closed a physical

48

circle, if not an emotional one, by settling in California, in Santa Barbara. At the same time I took up my lifelong tenancy in the bare muffled room of the professional writer where I am sitting now, with my back to the window, writing longhand in a Spiral notebook.

After ten years this writing routine was broken by circumstances which my later books more than adequately suggest. My wife and I lived in the San Francisco area for a year, and then came back to Santa Barbara. We rented a house on a cliff overlooking the sea and lived in it for a winter and a summer.

The Pacific had always lapped like blue eternity at the far edge of my life. The tides of that winter brought in old memories, some of which had drifted for forty years. In 1919, I remembered, my sea-captain father took me on a brief voyage and showed me a shining oceanic world from which I had felt exiled ever since, even during my sea duty in the Navy.

Exile and half-recovery and partial return had been the themes of at least two earlier books, *Blue City* and *The Three Roads* (which got its title from *Oedipus Tryannos*). I wrote them in 1946, the year I left the Navy and came back to California after my long absence. These novels borrowed some strength from my return to my native state but they missed the uniquely personal heart of the matter—matter which I will call Oedipal, in memory of that Theban who was exiled more than once.

In the red Spiral notebook where I set down my first notes for *The Galton Case*, Oedipus made an appropriately early appearance. His ancient name was surrounded by a profusion of ideas and images which I can see in retrospect were sketching out the groundwork for the novel. A crude early description of its protagonist turns up in two lines of verse about a tragicomic track meet:

> *A burst of speed! Half angel and half ape,*
> *The youthful winner strangles on the tape.*

Two Lines from another abortive poem—

> *Birds in the morning, scattered atomies:*
> *The voice is one, the voice is not my own.—*

49

were to supply an important detail to the closing page of the completed novel. The morning birds appear there as reminders of a world which encloses and outlasts the merely human.

A third and final example of these multitudinous early notes is one for an unwritten story—" 'The Fortieth Year' (downgrade reversed by an act of will)"—which recalls my then recent age and condition and suggests another character in the novel, the poet Chad Bolling. This middle-aged San Francisco poet is at the same time an object of parody and my spokesman for the possibilities of California life. Bolling's involvement in the Galton case takes him back to a sea cliff which he had visited as a young man, and he recovers some of a young man's high spirits:

> He flapped his arms some more. "I can fly! I breast the windy currents of the sky. I soar like Icarus toward the sun. The wax melts. I fall from a great height into the sea. Mother Thalassa."
> "Mother who?"
> "Thalassa, the sea, the Homeric sea. We could build another Athens. I used to think we could do it in San Francisco, build a new city of man on the great hills. A city measured with forgiveness. Oh, well."

Not long after this outburst, Bolling sits down to write his best poem in years, as he says. While I am not a true poet, I am content to have Bolling represent me here. He shows the kite-flying exuberance of a man beginning a lucky piece of work, and speaks unashamedly for the epic impulse which almost all writers of fiction try to service in some degree.

It was a complex business, getting ready to write even this moderately ambitious novel. Dozens of ideas were going through my mind in search of an organizing principle. The central idea which was to magnetize the others and set them in narrative order was a variation on the Oedipus story. It appears in the red notebook briefly and abruptly, without preparation: "Oedipus angry vs. parents for sending him away into a foreign country."

This simplification of the traditional Oedipus stories,

50

Sophoclean or Freudian, provides Oedipus with a conscious reason for turning against his father and suggests that the latter's death was probably not unintended. It rereads the myth through the lens of my own experience, and in this it is characteristic of my plots. Many of them are founded on ideas which question or invert or criticize received ideas and which could, if brevity were my forte, be expressed in aphorisms.

Neither plots nor characters can be borrowed, even from Freud or Sophocles. Like the moving chart of an encephalograph, the plot of a novel follows the curve of the mind's intention. The central character, and many of the other characters, are in varying degrees versions of the author. Flaubert said that he was Madam Bovary, William Styron that he became Nat Turner. The character holding the pen has to wrestle and conspire with the one taking shape on paper, extracting a vision of the self from internal darkness—a self dying into fiction as it comes to birth.

My mind had been haunted for years by an imaginary boy whom I recognized as the darker side of my own remembered boyhood. By his sixteenth year he had lived in fifty houses and committed the sin of poverty in each of them. I couldn't think of him without anger and guilt.

This boy became the central figure of *The Galton Case*. His nature and the nature of his story are suggested by some early titles set down in the red notebook: "A Matter of Identity," "The Castle and the Poorhouse," "The Impostor." He is, to put it briefly and rather inexactly, a false claimant, a poorhouse graduate trying to lie his way into the castle.

"The Castle and the Poorhouse," old-fashioned and melodramatic as the phrase is, accurately reflects the vision of the world which my adult imagination inherited from my childhood. It was a world profoundly divided, between the rich and the poor, the upright and the downcast, the sheep and the goats. We goats knew the moral pain inflicted not so much by poverty as by the doctrine, still current, that poverty is always deserved.

In the first winters of the Depression in Ontario, skilled factory workers were willing to put in a full week on piecework for as little as five dollars. The year I left high school, 1932, I was glad to work on a farm for my board alone. Healthy as that

51

year of farm life was, it was a year of waiting without much hope. I shared with many others the dilemma of finding myself to be at the same time two radically different kinds of people, a pauper and a member of the middle class. The dilemma was deepened by my fear that I'd never make it to college, and by my feeling of exile, which my mother had cultivated by teaching me from early childhood that California was my birthplace and natural home.

Such personal dilemmas tend to solidify along traditional philosophic lines. In a puritanical society the poor and fatherless, suffering the quiet punishments of despair, may see themselves as permanently and justifiably damned for crimes they can't remember having committed.

The Platonic split between more worthy and less worthy substances, idea and matter, spirit and flesh, widens under pressure. The crude pseudo-Darwinian dualism of my own phrase, "half angel and half ape," suggests an image of man not only divided but at war.

The Galton Case was an attempt to mend such gross divisions on the imaginative level. It tried to bring the Monster and the Laughing Boy into unity or congruence at least, and build a bridge, or a tunnel, between the poorhouse and the castle.

The castle is represented by the Galton family's Southern California estate, described as if it was literally a medieval demesne: "The majestic iron gates gave a portcullis effect. A serf who was cutting the lawn with a power-mower paused to tug at his forelock as we went by." The old widow who presides over this estate had quarreled with her son Anthony some twenty years ago, and Anthony had walked out and disappeared. Now Mrs. Galton has begun to dream of a reconciliation with her son. Through her attorney she hires the detective Lew Archer to look for him.

My earliest note on Anthony Galton will give an idea of his place in the story. A very young man and a poet, Anthony deliberately declassed himself in an effort, the note says, "to put together 'the castle and the poorhouse.' He changed his name (to John Brown) and became a workingman . . . Married under his pseudonym, to the common law wife of a man in jail," he was murdered when the other man got out.

About one-third of the way through the novel, the detective Archer is shown an incomplete set of human bones which prove to be Anthony Galton's. At the same time and the same place—not many miles up the coast from the Northern California town where I was born—Archer finds or is found by a boy who represents himself as Anthony's son and calls himself John Brown. The rest of the novel is concerned with this boy and his identity.

Perhaps I have encouraged the reader to identify this boy with me. If so, I must qualify that notion. The connections between a writer and his fiction, which are turning out to be my present subject, are everything but simple. My nature is probably better represented by the whole book than by any one of its characters. At the same time John Brown, Jr.'s life is a version of my early life: the former could not have existed without the latter.

The extent of this symbiosis can be seen in the two false starts I made on the novel, more clearly than in the finished product, where personal concerns were continually reshaped by overriding artistic needs. The most striking fact about these early versions is that they begin the story approximately where the completed novel ends it. Both Version One and Version Two, as I'll call them, are narrated by a boy who recalls aspects of my Canadian boyhood. The other characters including the father and mother are imaginary, as they are in the published novel.

In Version One the narrator's name is Tom. He lives on the poorer side of London, Ontario (where I attended university and in a sense graduated from the "poorhouse" of my childhood). Tom has finished high school but has no prospects. At the moment he is playing semi-pro pool.

He is challenged to a game by an American named Dawson who wears an expensive suit with a red pin-stripe in it. Tom wins easily and sees, when Dawson pays, that his wallet is "thick with money—American money, which always seems a little bit like stage money to me." From the standpoint of a poor Canadian boy, the United States and its riches seem unreal.

Tom has a taste for unreality. He had done some acting in high school, he tells Dawson.

53

"Did you enjoy acting"
Did I? It was the only time I ever felt alive,
when I could forget myself and the hole I lived
in, and turn into an imaginary character. "I
liked it, yeah."

Tom is not speaking for me here. I don't like acting. But it is probably not a coincidence that the American, Dawson, is a Ph.D. trained, as I was trained at the University of Toronto, "in the evaluation of intelligence."

Dawson is testing the boy's memory and acting ability and talking vaguely about hiring him, as Version One died in mid-sentence on its thirteenth page. This version suffered from lack of adequate planning, and from the associated difficulty of telling the boy's complicated story in his own simple person. Neither structure nor style was complex enough to let me discover my largely undiscovered purposes.

But immediately I made a second stab at having the boy narrate his own story. His name is Willie now, and he lives in Toronto, almost as if he was following in my footsteps. He has an appointment with an American, now named Mr. Sablacan, who is waiting for him at the Royal York Hotel.

Willie never gets there. All of Version Two takes place in his home, in the early morning. This rather roughly written six-page scene breaks the ground for my book and introduces some of its underlying themes: the hostility between father and son, for instance, here brought to an extreme pitch:

> *The old man was sitting at the kitchen table*
> *when I went down. He looked like a ghost with*
> *a two-day beard. The whole room stank of*
> *wine, and he was holding a partly empty bottle*
> *propped up between his crotch.*
> *. . . I kept one eye on him while I made break-*
> *fast.*
> *. . .He wouldn't throw the bottle as long as it*
> *had wine in it. After that, you never knew.*

The shades of Huck Finn and his father are pretty well dispel-led, I think, when the boy's mother comes down. She approaches her drunken husband "with that silly adoring look on her face, as if he was God Almighty giving her a break just by letting her live. 'You've been working and thinking all night,' she said. 'Your poor head needs a rest. I'll fix you a nice cup of tea . . .' "

Later, she stops an argument between the father and the boy by silencing the father.

> *He sat in his chair and looked down into his bottle. You'd think from the expression on his face that it was a telescope which let him see all the way down to hell. All of a sudden his face went slack. He went to sleep in his chair. The old lady took the bottle away from him as if he was a baby . . .*
> *. . . I sat and ate my breakfast in silence. With the old man propped up opposite me, eyes closed and mouth open, it was a little like eating with a dead man at the table.*

My story had begun to feed on its Oedipal roots, both mythical and psychological. Relieved by the mother of his crotch-held bottle, the father has undergone symbolic death. The short scene ends with the boy's determination to get away not only from his father but from his mother:

> *She'd go on feeding me until I choked. She'd be pouring me cups of tea until I drowned in the stuff. She'd give me loving encouragement until I suffocated.*

Version Two was a good deal more than a false start. Swarming with spontaneous symbolism, it laid out one whole side, the sinister side, of the binocular vision of my book. In fact it laid it out so completely that it left me, like Willie, nowhere to go but away. I couldn't begin the novel with the infernal vision on which part of its weight would finally rest; the novel must converge on that gradually. But by writing my last scene first, in effect, and facing its Medusa images—poverty and family failure and hostility—my imagination freed itself to plan the novel without succumbing to the more obvious evasions.

Even so, as I was trying to finish the first draft, I got morally tired and lost my grip on my subject, ending the book with a dying fall in Nevada. My friend John Mersereau read this draft—entitled, appropriately, "The Enormous Detour"—and reminded me that a book like mine could not succeed as a novel unless it succeeded in its own terms as a detective novel. For my ending I went back to Version Two, which contains the dramatic essence of the final confrontations. Willie's scene with his parents served me well, leading me into the heart of my subject not just once but again.

A second break-through at the beginning, more technical and less obviously important, came with my decision to use the detective Archer as the narrator. This may seem a small matter, but it was not. The decision on narrative point-of-view is a key one for any novelist. It determines shape and tone, and even the class of detail that can be used. With this decision I made up my mind that the convention of the detective novel, in which I had been working for fifteen years, would be able to contain the materials of my most ambitious and personal work so far. I doubt that my book could have been written in any other form.

Miss Brigid Brophy has alleged against the detective story that it cannot be taken seriously because it fails to risk the author's ego and is therefore mere fantasy. It is true as I have noted that writers since Poe have used detectives like Dupin as a sort of rational strong point from which they can observe and report on a violent no-man's-land. Unfortunately this violent world is not always fantastic, although it may reflect psychological elements. Miss Brophy's argument disregards the fact that the detective and his story can become means of knowing oneself and saying the unsayable. You can never hit a distant target by aiming at it directly.

In any case I have to plead not guilty to unearned security of the ego. As I write a book, as I wrote *The Galton Case*, my ego is dispersed through several characters, including usually some of the undesirable ones, and I am involved with them to the limit of my imaginative strength. In modern fiction the narrator is not always the protagonist or hero, nor is the protagonist always single. Certainly my narrator Archer is not the main object of my interest, nor the character with whose fate I am most concerned. He is a deliberately narrowed version of the writing self, so narrow that when he turns sideways he almost disappears. Yet his semi-transparent presence places the story at one remove from the author and lets it, as we say (through sweat and tears), write itself.

I remember the rush of invention that occurred when the emotional and imaginative urges, the things *The Galton Case* was to be about, were released by Willie's scene with his parents, and channeled by my decision to write the book from Archer's point of view. The details came unbidden in a benign avalanche which in two or three days filled the rest of the red notebook. The people and the places weren't all final, but they were definte enough to let me begin the wild masonry of laying detail on detail to make a structure. (Naturally many of the details came in already organized gestalts: people in relationship, events in narrative order.)

Detective novels differ from some other kinds of novel, in having to have a rather hard structure built in logical coherence. But the structure will fail to satisfy the mind, writer's or reader's, unless the logic of imagination, tempered by feelings and rooted in the unconscious, is tied to it, often subverting it. The plans for a detective novel in the making are less like blueprints than like travel notes set down as you once revisited a city. The city had changed since you saw it last. It keeps changing around you. Some of the people you knew there have changed their names. Some of them wear disguises.

Take for example Dr. Dawson who lost a game of pool to Tom in Version One and became, in Version Two, a Mr. Sablacan waiting for Willie at the Royal York. In my final notes and in the novel itself he has become Gordon Sable, identifiable with his earlier personae by his name and by the fact that, like Dr. Dawson, he wears a suit with a wicked red pin-stripe in it. His occupation has changed, and his function in the novel has expanded. Gordon Sable is the attorney who hires Lew Archer on Mrs. Galton's behalf to look for her lost son Anthony.

Archer and Gordon Sable know each other. The nature of their relationship is hinted at by a small incident on the first page of the novel. A line of it will illustrate some of the implications of style, which could be described as structure on a small scale. Archer sits down on a Harvard chair in Gordon Sable's office, and then gets up. "It was like being expelled."

In a world of rich and poor, educated and disadvantaged, Archer's dry little joke places him on the side of the underdog. It suggests that he is the kind of man who would sympathize with the boy impostor waiting in the wings. And of course it speaks for the author—my own application for a graduate fellowship at Harvard was turned down thirty years ago—so that like nearly everything in fiction the joke has a private side which partly accounts for its having been made. The University of Michigan gave me a graduate fellowship in 1941, by the way, and my debt to Ann Arbor is duly if strangely acknowledged in the course of John Brown, Jr's. story.

Detective stories are told backward, as well as forward, and full revelation of the characters and their lives' meanings is deferred until the end, or near the end. But even deeper structural considerations require the main dynamic elements of a story to be laid in early. For this and other reasons, such as the further weight and dimension imparted by repetition, it is sometimes a good idea to let a character and his story divide. One part or aspect of him can perform an early function in the story which foreshadows the function of his later persona, without revealing too much of it.

John Brown, Jr., as I've already said, doesn't enter the story until it is one-third told. I decided, though hardly on the fully conscious level, to provide John with a stand-in or alter ego to pull his weight in the early part of the narrative. When I invented this other boy, and named him Tom Lemberg, I had totally forgotten that Tom was the name of the boy in Version One who beat Dr. Dawson at pool. But here he is in the novel: an earlier stage in the development of my boy impostor. A specimen of fiction, like a biological specimen, seems to recapitulate the lower stages of its evolution. I suspect Tom had to be brought in to validate my novel, proving that I had touched in order all the bases between life and fiction. At any rate the book comes alive when Archer and Tom Lemberg, two widely distinct versions of the author, confront each other in Chapter Five.

This confrontation with Tom of course prefigures Archer's confrontation with the boy impostor John. Tom serves an even more important purpose at the beginning of the book, when he is held responsible for the murder of Peter Culligan. The structure of the story sufficiently identifies Culligan with the wino father, so that Culligan's death parallels and anticipates the final catastrophe. Like the repeated exile of Oedipus, the crucial events of my novel seem to happen at least twice. And like a young Oedipus, Tom is a "son" who appears to kill a "father," thus setting the whole story in circular motion.

I have told a little too much of that story for comfort, and a little too much of my own story. One final connection between the private story and the public one should suffice. When Archer opens the dead Culligan's suitcase, "Its contents emitted a whiff of tobacco, sea water, sweat, and the subtler indescribable odor of masculine loneliness." These were the smells, as I remembered and imagined them, of the pipe-smoking sea-captain who left my mother and me when I was about the age that grandson Jimmie was when he became a monster in my poor castle, and then a laughing boy, and fell asleep.

11

From South Dakota Review

KNOWING EXACTLY WHERE he is is as important to a writer as it is to a blind man. To most of us, loss of place is as radical as loss of vision: we seem to be able to see only what we know. Many of my fictional characters seem to be lost on this continent, and I suspect that their experiences are partly autobiographical.

I am both literally and imaginatively a biped, resting one uneasy foot in California where I was born and have spent the best part of my adult life, and the other foot in Canada where I was raised and partly educated. This geographical range and stretch account for some of the peculiarities of my work. Many of my plots originate in the north and the middle west, as I did, but tend to end (as I have) in California. This temporal span, which often approximates a lifetime, seems to reflect the time it took me to put together the places and their meanings, if I have.

The main stories generally begin and end in the open self-inviting society of California, but there outcomes are determined, predetermined, by an ethical and psychological causality which I associate with my forebears in the north, Mennonite and Presbyterian. The Californian escapists of my books drag with them their whole pasts, rattling like chains among the castanets.

To one who first came to consciousness in British Columbia and to maturity in California, the most persistent place, or thing, is the Pacific Ocean and its shores. This ocean, with its great spatial and temporal continuities, its currents and recurrences, its destructions and renewals, represents a changing constant in my life and fiction. It is the nearest thing in my fiction to an inescapable and memorable place. My sailor father plied its waters in the first world war and I traveled them in the second. I live within sight of the Pacific and wet myself in it nearly every day.

Just beyond the mountains which form the other horizon of my world, Canada seems to hang like a glacier slowly moving down on me from its notch. I expect it to overtake me before I die, reminding me with its chill and weight that I belong to the north after all.

We writers never leave the places where our first lasting memories begin and have names put to them. Together with our culture and our genes, both of which are in some sense the outgrowth of place, these places seem to constitute our fate. Our whole lives move along their ancient trails. But even when we are standing neck-deep in the open graves of our past we scan the horizon for new places, new possibilities. And as the final shovelsful plop down onto our faces we taste in the dirt that chokes our mouths the spores of another promised land.

12

A Death Road for the Condor

W E ATE LUNCH on top of Big Pine. It was a brilliantly clear day and from this elevation, 6,800 feet, we could look down over the Coast Range, across the Santa Barbara Channel, and see all of the Channel Islands. In the other direction, inland, the Mount Wilson group stood under December snow. Farther north loomed the white peaks of Yosemite.

We took quick bites of our sandwiches and scanned the nearer horizons with our binoculars. This was condor country. At the foot of Big Pine lies the San Rafael Primitive Area, one of our few remaining wildernesses, and at its northern edge is the Sisquoc Condor Sanctuary. The Sierra Madre Ridge above the sanctuary is a major condor flyway, and has been since prehistoric times. But today there was not a condor in the sky.

The Forest Supervisor and his Assistant looked at us over their lunches with I-told-you-so expressions.

"There are practically no condors in the area anymore," said the Supervisor.

"Our observers see them all the time," I said.

The Supervisor's Assistant said firmly: "Our observers practically never see one."

The Supervisor and his Assistant didn't seem to want to see any condors, I thought. Their reluctance would have to do with the project they were pushing at the moment: the development of a through road along the Sierra Madre Ridge. They had brought us conservationists and bird watchers along on the present expedition in an effort to persuade us that the building of the Sierra Madre road and the consequent opening of the backcountry to cars and motorcycles would damage neither the wilderness nor the condors, if any.

The Supervisor rose athletically from his rock, a handsome man, extraordinarily tall, with clipped iron-gray hair and quick, boyish smile. His Assistant was shorter and broader, but very alert-looking. They reminded me of a brigadier general and his aide, shortly after the general has decided to run for public office.

"If you men have finished eating," the Supervisor said, "we can be on our way."

"But don't let us rush you," said the Assistant Supervisor.

They were important people who liked to be liked. The Supervisor managed two million acres of national forest, including nearly half of Santa Barbara County. If he wanted to build a road along the edge of his wilderness and open it up to Los Angeles Sunday traffic, he was going to be hard to stop. And he definitely wanted to build it. He and his rangers were openly advocating the road, in chambers of commerce and service clubs and rifle clubs.

The Forest Service, once noted for its single-minded idealism, has developed in recent years an interest in the art of politics and the manipulation of public opinion. The Supervisor's Assistant had confided to me on the way up to Big Pine that knowledge of human beings was his most valuable asset as a career forester. Soon, if he handled people properly, he would have a forest of his own.

Now, as we drove down from Big Pine, we argued about the road.

"We need it for fire fighting," he said.

"You've got a primitive fire road along the ridge, which has always been adequate. You haven't had a fire there in nearly 40 years."

"Are you an expert on fire fighting?"

"No, but I can read, and I know what your own experts are saying. Fire fighting is taking more and more to the air, using borate bombers and, eventually, missiles. Ask your missile research division. Or ask Keith Arnold, your forest protection research director, what happens to the fire risk when you let increasing numbers of people into a forest area."

He admitted that the risk rose. "But we have no right to keep the people out. The road will be built with public money, and that makes it public property."

"The condors and the wilderness are public property, too. They belong to the whole country."

"But this road," he said with esthetic fervor, "would make a beautiful scenic drive. We could have picnic grounds along it, too."

"You can't have a scenic drive and a wilderness area within five miles of each other. You'd be putting the Sisquoc Sanctuary, the heart of the wilderness, within two hours' hiking time of an automobile road, half an hour by motorcycle. You'll ruin your wilderness and drive away your condors."

"The condors hardly use the Sisquoc anymore."

"So you keep saying. Our people see them there constantly. It's a roosting area and a former nesting site that the birds can use again if anything happens to their alternate sites. The Falls of the Sisquoc is still their best watering place."

The Assistant Supervisor was not impressed. "So what? Who says the road will bother them?"

"All the experts say so. The condors are allergic to road building and automobiles and people in any great numbers."

"Five or six or seven miles away?"

"Yes. And remember they don't just sit on the Sisquoc. The Sierra Madre Ridge is their flyway. This whole backcountry is their range."

I waved my arm rather emotionally out the car window. We were on the Buckhorn Road, headed north toward the Sierra Madre Ridge. The canyons and ridges of the wilderness lay around us like a violent dark green sea quick-frozen. It had been frozen in time. Except for the road we were on, a fire road normally closed to automobiles, nothing had changed here in 2,000 years.

The condor had been flying here longer than that, I thought. He had been catching the updrafts along these ridges since the Pleistocene Age. He was ancient. He was great, the greatest flying land bird in North America. His wingspan often exceeded nine feet. He could fly up to 50 miles an hour, scarcely moving his wings, with or against the wind, all day if necessary.

Aeronautical engineers studied his design. Naturalists came from all over the world to catch a glimpse of him.

He was harmless and useful. He cleared the rangeland of dead animals. With only about 50 of him left, there was no lack of food. But he was running out of space to nest and roost. His range, which had once extended from ocean to ocean and from the Columbia River south to Mexico, had shrunk now to this small part of California.

We were only a few miles from his last retreats on the Sisquoc and the Sespe. We still hadn't seen him. I was getting anxious.

The Buckhorn Road is primitive and seldom used, even by Forest Service automobiles. From time to time our party had to stop and push fallen boulders out of the way of our cars. They rumbled down into the canyon.

Following the dust smoke of one such boulder, I caught sight of a little black thing half a mile or more down the precipitous slope. The little thing seemed to be crawling up over the secondary ridges, like a black beetle with extended wings. Then I saw that he was crawling above the ground, in midair, rising in air and growing steadily and incredibly larger.

I didn't speak. I didn't even raise my binoculars. Poised and outspread on the updraft, emblem and living totem of wilderness men and flyers, he rose up the slope toward me. Now I could see the clean white epaulets on his black shoulders and make out with my naked eye the deep orange color of his bald head. At his wingtips the great black primary feathers curved up individually in the wind. He balanced in the air a hundred yards away from where we stood, regarding us with his glistening black eye. Then he wheeled, the undersides of his wings glinting white in the sun, and slid away.

I think we all saw him, except the Supervisor and possibly the Supervisor's Assistant, who didn't say.

That was back in December. On February 27 the Forest Service held a public meeting in Santa Barbara. It was presided over by the Regional Forester, an elderly gentleman who looked like a major general but who described himself as a bureaucrat.

He watched with a calm, cold eye while the Forest Service's road project was severely criticized by conservationists, including me and my wife, and by a number of experts in the fields of botany, ornithology and land use. Proponents of the road seemed to feel that they were being undemocratically excluded from the wilderness, though everyone, including the Forest Service, knows that a wilderness area, like a woman, loses its character permanently if it is visited by too many lovers.

One ardent proponent of the road suggested that condor lovers might keep a few stuffed condors around town that they could love. This one made even the Regional Forester look uncomfortable. But at the end of the meeting he stated that there were extremists on both sides and that his decision would fall between the two extremes. Which seemed to imply that he would decide to ruin the wilderness just a little, for the present, and permit the condor to survive for a few more years, perhaps.

The Supervisor's Assistant spoke to me on the way out of the meeting. "Another day," he said cheerfully.

On March 21 the Regional Forester announced that he would defer his decision on building the road until its effect on the survival of the condor had been studied further.

13

Life With The Blob

THE BLOB five miles offshore had been growing for 24 hours before Santa Barbara, Calif. knew about it. Then, on Wednesday morning, an oil worker called the city editor of the *News-Press*. He said the new well being drilled on Union's Platform A had blown out the day before and was still blowing.

Tom Kleveland, a gray-haired columnist who acts as a local ombudsman, went out in a workboat to look at it. A thick surge of crude oil smothered the sea around the platform. Oil and large gas bubbles were coming up in at least five places, lifting the surface of the water two feet. "It looked like a big yellow boil bursting with pus," Tom told me later.

Our evening paper confirmed the disaster. Margaret and I went out on the patio and looked across the channel to the islands, 25 miles offshore. The soft blue scene seemed intact. But there was a difference in the light—or in our vision of it—now that we knew it was threatened and perishable.

Though we couldn't see the oil platforms through the narrow mouth of our canyon, we had been steadily aware of them. Their coming over the past year had brought a sense of impending change to Santa Barbara, to our beaches and our sea and our eggshell-fragile way of life. Offshore in the quiet evening the change was taking place, and there was nothing we could do about it.

"This could be another *Torrey Canyon*, couldn't it? How many seabirds did that kill?"

I turned my wife's question aside. "A ruptured oil well isn't the same as a wrecked tanker. They may get it capped right away." I had just read in the paper that Union Oil's regional vice-president, John Fraser, had assured city officials that the spill should be under control or completely stopped within 24 hours.

The oil was still running uncontrolled on Saturday. Margaret and I went to a protest rally at East Beach, instigated by a group who called themselves GOO (Get Oil Out). One of their leaders, former State Senator Al Weingand, made a disturbing speech.

Several years before, he had flown over the channel and the islands with Secretary of the Interior Stewart L. Udall. Both men were interested in creating a Channel Islands National Park. Weingand had asked Udall for assurances against oil pollution. "No oil leases will be granted," the Secretary had promised, "except under conditions that will protect your environment."

But in spite of this assurance, the oil rigs had gathered offshore like a slow invasion fleet. The oil pumping had begun—and now it continued, even though the ocean floor had been hemorrhaging for four days. One mile of our beaches to the south had already been flooded with the black tarry stuff.

East Beach was still untouched. Sanderlings ran in close groups like shimmering gravel. Black cormorants flew low over the untainted white surf. But Margaret and I were living in suspense. Our region is a natural bird sanctuary surpassed by no more than four or five other places in the country. Scientists at the University of California's Santa Barbara campus were already predicting heavy losses. Biologist John Cushing was particularly concerned about the seabirds, which swallowed oil as they preened themselves and were often poisoned by it.

We didn't know how much oil was out there. Union Oil's estimates of the spillage were quite low: its initially quoted estimate (subsequently denied) of 5,000 barrels a day was later down to 500 barrels a day. But according to Alan A. Allen, a scientist with the General Research Corp. who regularly flew over the spill, at least 20,000 barrels of oil were floating just offshore.

On Sunday the wind rose. It blew seaward and kept the oil off our beaches, lulling all of us with foolish hope. The new Secretary of the Interior, Walter Hickel, came out from Washington on Sunday, and after a flight over the channel asked the oil companies to stop drilling voluntarily. But within 24 hours Hickel gave the companies permission to resume operation.

By 5 o'clock of that same afternoon the oil was coming in on our public beaches. It lay so thick on the water that the waves were unformed; they made a squishing sound. The next morning the harbor was full of oil. Fishermen and yachtsmen stood around, looking at the black water and the blackened hulls of their boats.

Toward evening I paid a visit to the shore nearest our home, Hope Ranch Beach. There I found something at the edge of the water that looked like a caricature of a western grebe modeled in tar. I tried to catch the poor black flopping thing. It struggled into the water and dived, or sank.

The smell of oil followed me up the canyon to our house, a mile from the sea. The smell, I thought, was beginning to flavor our lives. And we began to get some sense of the scope of our disaster. Ian McMillan, a noted wildlife expert, had come to town on behalf of The Defenders of Wildlife and made an aerial survey of the channel. Afterward, we had lunch together. Ian reported that the affected area was much greater than the Coast Guard's latest estimate, which was 200 square miles. But that was only the solid oil slick. Ian said more like 800 square miles were polluted, and he later increased his estimate to 1,200 square miles.

Though he is a world authority on the California condor, Ian more closely resembles an eagle. A screaming eagle note entered his voice when he began to explain the damage to marine life and birds. "Once the birds are oiled, there isn't much use trying to save them," he said. "They don't do well in captivity. Even if we manage to keep some alive for a time, it's difficult to release them back to the wild. The effects of the spill won't easily be undone, and I deplore"—his voice rose—"I deplore attempts to play it down. I talked to some State Fish and Game men at the harbor this morning. They said they had counted a total of 126 dead birds and rescued 108 live ones. This is just local and immediate damage, as they ought to know if they don't. But they're putting these figures out as official information. Meanwhile hundreds and probably thousands of birds are dying out at sea or being buried on the beaches."

That night an editor of *The New York Times,* who is a fellow birder, called from Washington and asked me what I would look for if I were there in his place. I said I would try to find out how the decision ever got made—under a conservationist Interior Secretary like Udall—to sell oil-drilling leases in a geologically unstable channel between a projected national park and a coastline that was famous for its beauty. For further light on the question I referred my editor friend to ex-Senator Weingand.

Part of the answer came out in the Sunday *Times.* Udall had been reached in Phoenix and took responsibility for the decision. He added that there had been "no dissent" in the Interior Department, "because 12 years of experience in the Gulf of Mexico, off Louisiana and Texas, had not led to any big leaks, even during hurricanes."

This was strangely in conflict with the statements of an employee of Red Adair, the Houston expert on capping wild oil wells, whose team had been called in to control the Santa Barbara spill. He said that spills were so common off Louisiana that they seldom got into the newspapers. And a Santa Barbara teacher, Fred Eissler, revealed that Udall's account of the decision-making process needed further correction. As a national director of the Sierra Club, Eissler had corresponded with Udall during the battle against the oil rigs coming into our channel. He produced a memo written by Stanley A. Cain, an ecologist who was Udall's Assistant Secretary for fish, wildlife and parks. On Aug. 7, 1967, Dr. Cain came out in favor of making the Santa Barbara Channel a marine sanctuary. Several days later, under pressure from the Budget Bureau and after a talk with J. Cordell Moore, the Assistant Secretary in charge of mineral resources, Dr. Cain reversed himself.

As the pieces of the story gradually came together, they seemed to show that the decision was made in favor of oil in the channel, and $603 million of lease money in the U.S. Treasury, without any realistic concern for the local consequences. Dr. Cain wrote in his second memo, for instance, that the oil rigs would stand no closer than five miles to the shore, and that this "would certainly reduce platform visibility from land to neg-

72

ligibility." The fact is that, at the guaranteed distance, the 200-foot drilling structures loom up about as invisibly as aircraft carriers in the channel. I was told by a colleague of Dr. Cain's that the Assistant Secretary was originally a botanist who had done work on tropical vegetation.

Meanwhile, Secretary Hickel was under mounting pressure to stop the oil operations in the channel. The youngest and fieriest of Santa Barbara County's five supervisors, George Clyde, told Edmund Muskie's U.S. Senate Subcommittee on Air and Water Pollution that Secretary Hickel's 24-hour moratorium on oil drilling was "tokenism" that "smacks of cynicism and cold hypocrisy." Charles M. Teague, the conservative Congressman from our district, asked Hickel to reconsider his rapid decision and later introduced a bill to stop the drilling permanently.

One of the voices raised in Washington in defense of drilling belonged to Fred L. Hartley, president of the Union Oil Co. He assured Senator Muskie and his subcommittee that his firm exercised "reasonable diligence" in its drilling. He talked like a man on whom the Santa Barbara Channel had played a dirty trick. His general explanation of the blowout—"Mother Nature, if you have had much contact with her, you will find is always teaching new things"—immediately made Mr. Hartley our favorite natural philosopher.

Within 48 hours we had an unexpected chance to meet him. Senator Muskie and Senator Alan Cranston of California flew out to Santa Barbara for an on-the-spot hearing. Several hundred local people went to the airport to greet them, carrying signs, including Margaret's own BAN THE BLOB. Just ahead of the Senators' plane a blue-and-orange Union Oil jet landed. Out stepped Mr. Hartley, a heavyset man with a commanding eye. Many of us booed him, not so much for ruining our coast as for treating us like natives who could be quieted by the techniques of public relations.

Mr. Hartley, followed by several reporters, walked up to me and angrily demanded my name. I gave it to him and added for the benefit of the reporters that I was secretary of the Scenic Shoreline Preservation Conference. Mr. Hartley muttered, "That was quite a speech," and stalked away. I wondered why he had chosen me for his attentions. Margaret said that Mr. Hartley appeared to be accident prone.

Mr. Hartley's impatience carried over into the subcommittee hearing, which was held in the supervisors' meeting room before a packed house. He told Senator Muskie and us that our common disaster was not a disaster, on the grounds that no human beings had been killed. We groaned. Mr. Hartley did have one cheering thing to say. Now, in the 11th day of the spill, his company had assembled enough drilling mud and cement to stop the leaks in the ocean floor, it hoped. The headline in the next day's paper—LEAK PLUGGED, SAYS UNION OIL—made some of us let out a sigh of relief. Others, mostly geologists and oilmen, waited for the other shoe to drop.

Secretary Hickel, yielding finally to public or presidential pressure, had ordered the suspension of all federal oil operations in the Santa Barbara Channel. Because of the danger of further spills, most of us were determined to make the suspension permanent. Over the weekend hundreds of petition bearers spread out over the county. Margaret and I set up a table on Cabrillo Boulevard near the beach to catch the people from out of town.

Cabrillo Boulevard hadn't been so crowded with sightseers since the Fiesta in August. Most of the visitors at our Black Fiesta were glad to sign our Get Oil Out petition. A couple of embarrassed oil workers admitted to "mixed feelings." A few others, even some who signed, advised us gravely that we were wasting our time: the oil companies were too big to fight.

We didn't believe that, and neither did Supervisor George Clyde. He announced over the weekend that he would ask the other supervisors to join him in a resolution against all oil-drilling operations off county shores. On Monday it was passed unanimously before a standing-room-only crowd of citizens. As Supervisor Joe Callahan said, Santa Barbara hadn't been so united since the great earthquake of 1925—which just about wiped the town out.

In the middle of the week I spot-checked 20 miles of beaches to get an idea of the present damage, which was occurring in spite of the considerable efforts of Union Oil to keep the oil off shore and clean up the pollution. I saw no more than a dozen birds, and only three or four of them were shorebirds.

Carpinteria Beach was a black wasteland. Just back of it I found a bird rescue station that Union Oil had set up, and was guided through the two trailers that housed it by a pleasant young man in coveralls. The open plywood pens were full of diving birds, mostly western grebes and loons, sea ducks and cormorants. The hard-hatted oil engineers who looked after them had given each bird the same treatment: a pat of butter forced down its throat to clean it out, a bath of dispersant (Polycomplex A-11), a warm place to sit and pieces of fish to eat.

Of the 600 birds rescued in the 15 days since the well first blew, some 60% had survived. I didn't have the heart to tell the engineers that one month after the *Torrey Canyon* spill, of 7,849 birds rescued only 450 survived, and many of these died later, or that, according to English ornithologist James Fisher, for every bird washed ashore at least one was lost at sea.

I visited another bird rescue station, this one at the children's zoo in Santa Barbara. A pretty blonde girl wearing a smock told me in a soft Australian accent that her station had cared for more than 400 birds, of which more than half had died. She was able to show me one shorebird, a rather frazzled godwit standing under a heat lamp. I asked her if the shorebirds had gone inland. She didn't know. But on my way home I stopped at Shoreline Park, above the beach, and counted six oil-smudged sanderlings foraging in the grass.

When I walked into the house Margaret silently handed me the evening paper. The headline said: OIL IS FLOWING AGAIN FROM CHANNEL RUPTURE. We decided to have a look, and reserved a plane for the next day. Then we lined up several expert observers, including a naturalist-photographer, Dick Smith; a writer, Robert Easton; and Waldo Abbott, the ornithologist of the Santa Barbara Museum of Natural History.

The pilot, Margaret Mead of Powderpuff Derby fame, flew us directly out over Platform A and circled the blue skyscraper several times. Oil was welling up in at least three places, coming to the surface on an east-west front of about 1,000 feet. I later found out from a geologist what this meant. "It's leaking along the line of the fault," he said, "which is bad. These multiple leaks are awfully hard to plug."

We flew due south to the mountainous island of Santa Cruz. Much of its shoreline had been blackened, and there was oil on the water far out to sea beyond it. Anacapa, a cliff-surrounded island that is small enough to be seen from the air all at once, was encircled by oil on the beaches and on the water. Anacapa is a national monument.

The last time I visited the island, the beaches had had a primeval quality. Surfbirds and black and ruddy turnstones had crouched on the wet rocks. A few black oyster catchers had poked at shellfish with their surreal red beaks. Now the only visible birds were the gulls speckling a sandbar. We sat in silence as our pilot turned back toward the mainland. The oil lay everywhere on the water in blobs and windrows and iridescent slicks.

Flying from Port Hueneme westward to Santa Barbara, we surveyed 45 miles of polluted beaches. The tide line was a broad black band that looked from the air like something marked on a map with a black crayon. Or, when we flew lower, a spattering black brush.

The simile was Waldo Abbott's. "The tide works like a paintbrush on the intertidal zone," he was saying. "It puts on a new coat of oil every time it comes in and recedes. It's hard on the smaller plants and animals—the things that the birds and the larger fishes live on." And then his mind moved in a swoop from the tiny world to the large one: "This is just a little sample of what could happen." He meant the next major earthquake that some seismologists said was overdue, the earthquake that could give us the ultimate oil bath.

The present one was enough. Over the weekend a southeaster rose, driving the floating oil in from the channel, dislodging it from the kelp beds and blowing it to the shore. Suddenly the Biltmore beach, which had already been cleaned by state prisoners and Union Oil men, now looked worse than it ever had, with oil flung 10 feet high along its seawall. Close offshore the sea was a brown emulsion plowed by one forlorn grebe.

Dr. Joseph H. Connell and other university scientists were studying the effects of this oil on life—both animal and human. So far the larger fishes seemed undamaged, though professionals had detected no significant schools of fish in the channel since the spill began. Some of the intertidal life, mussels and anemones, could live with the oil. But some other small species were not so durable. The damage to their populations might cause changes in the food chain, the consequences of which could not yet be measured.

76

I was particularly interested in the findings of two young environmental scientists, Dr. Norman K. Sanders and Dr. Robert R. Curry. For Sanders the disaster was mainly a human one. The danger, as he saw it, was that the degradation of the environment could ruin Santa Barbara's pride and turn it into just another technological slum. Dr. Curry considered an even more frightening danger: "We had more than 60 moderate earthquakes here last summer and they all originated in the channel. What happens when a major earthquake or a seismic wave comes along? Sooner or later one will. It could knock the whole thing over, shear off the wells if they're still there. The oil could run for years."

Curry is a young man of striking appearance and temperament, with black curly hair and flashing brown eyes. He is also widely qualified in geophysics, geology, hydrology and ecology. About 10 days after our conversation he testified as an expert witness before the Senate. Pointing out the dangers of further drilling in the channel, Curry concluded that "federal leases . . . should be revoked and the offshore fields declared petroleum reserves to be used only in the event of a national emergency." Failing that, the oil operations should be shut down "while the technology caught up to the need for safety." The Senators were so impressed that they hired Curry as an adviser.

It seemed to a layman that the Senators—and the Government—were in need of some new experts. Donald W. Solanas of the Interior Department, whose job it was to supervise our offshore oil operations, defended both the government's widely criticized drilling regulations and the activities of Union Oil. The company complied with the rules, he said, but "Mother Earth broke down on us." Mr. Solanas sounded as if he'd been studying natural philosophy with Mr. Hartley. But his former boss, Secretary Udall, now recognized the seismic dangers in the channel and confessed that he and other Interior Department officials had been "overconfident" in permitting oil drilling there.

Fred Eissler argued that the oil spill could have been averted if the government had listened to the objections of local people. (A high Interior Department official, Eugene W. Standley, had advised against a public hearing on the oil issue because it would "stir up the natives.") Now, Eissler told the subcommittee, the channel should be made into a marine sanctuary under legislation similar to the Wilderness Act.

Toward the end of the day, walking with Bob Easton in the foothills, I told him what had been said at the hearing. He had worked with Fred Eissler for years to get the San Rafael Wilderness established in Santa Barbara's backcountry. Now his imagination was touched by the idea of an ocean wilderness complementing our mountain wilderness and completed by a Channel Islands National Park.

We paused on Mountain Drive and looked out over the platform-studded sea. "It isn't enough just to get rid of them," Bob said. "We've got to convert this horror to positive good. Perhaps we can use it as a pivot to turn the country around before we completely wreck our living space."

On an afternoon near the end of the first month of the era of the Blob, Dr. Sanders brought his wife over to meet mine. By a nice coincidence, Gillian Sanders turned out to be the blonde Australian girl who cared for rescued birds at the children's zoo.

Norman Sanders belongs to a new academic breed. He is a tall, young outdoorsman who once flew the Alaska salmon patrol for the Fish and Wildlife Service and once attempted, with his wife, to sail his 20-foot boat eastward from Tasmania to California.

Now he talked about the necessity of saving our coast. "Some scientists are saying that before long we may not be able to live anywhere else—the interior will be completely polluted."

"Do you believe that could happen?"

"It could, unless we learn to use the planet without destroying it. Our society has failed miserably in letting this spill occur. What if Bob Curry's nightmare came true? What if Southern California lost all its sea life and its beaches? What would the people do?"

"Riot, maybe."

"I wouldn't be surprised. Degraded living conditions are a major source of unrest." Sanders paused in a listening attitude, as if he could hear distant rumblings. "There's just one positive thing about this oil mess. Until quite recently, it wouldn't have created such a national uproar. People are finally catching on to how much we have to lose, and how fast we're losing it."

As we talked, our wives moved in from an adjoining room. Margaret was telling Gillian that Hope Ranch Beach had been less severely damaged than some others. The shorebirds were returning, and in spite of the ever-present blob, even a few western grebes could be seen offshore. So our own beach had been lucky. But dead and dying birds were still being picked up along 200 miles of shoreline.

I asked Gillian how her rescued birds at the zoo were doing. She answered with downcast eyes: "They're dying."

She took it hard. As her husband had said, the main disaster is ours. If the oil spillage is ever completely controlled, most of the birds and the other wildlife will eventually renew themselves. But the human damage is irreparable. Our ease and confidence in our environment has cracked, slightly but permanently, like an egg.

14

Black Tide
(adapted from Foreword to book by Robert Easton)

T HE ERUPTION OF THE OIL WELL on Union Platform A off Santa Barbara on January 28, 1969, has had profound effects, and could be described as the blowout heard around the world.

The blowout shook the industry and the federal bureaucracy, whose rules and safeguards had failed to prevent it, and is gradually forcing the reform of those rules and safeguards. It triggered a social movement and helped to create a new politics, the politics of ecology, which is likely to exert a decisive influence on future elections and on our lives. It brought to a head our moral and economic doubts about the American uses of energy and raised the question of whether we really have to go on polluting the sea and land and air in order to support our freeway philosophy of one man, one car.

In the early postwar years, Santa Barbara was a quiet seaport facing south across white public beaches to blue waters reflecting a clear sky. A boat trip to the Channel Islands was like a voyage to Eden. The channel was alive with fish and dolphins, sea lions, whales in season, birds on the water and in the air. There was so little traffic in town that traffic lights were unnecessary and I could ride my bicycle down the main street with my black dog Skipper carelessly trailing me. There was a sense of freedom and ease in the untainted atmosphere. The city had so many trees and gardens that it seemed to be interfused with live green nature.

Santa Barbara's tradition of living at respectful ease with

81

nature went back a long way. For a thousand years before the white man came, the Indians had built their villages on the coastal slope. They lived on acorns and fish, and decorated their ceremonial caves with some of the finest primitive art in the world. The Santa Barbara pueblo was founded by the Spanish in 1782, the year after Los Angeles. A gradual immigration from the east changed the graceful Spanish character of the city without destroying it, and strengthened it with rigor and independence of thought.

Santa Barbara became a center of West Coast civilization, a place that leading American writers knew and referred to in their books. Naturalists, impressed by the equable climate, transplanted flowers and trees from other continents. Santa Barbara's Museum of Natural History was founded by William L. Dawson, whose *Birds of California* is still the classic on that subject. The Museum, the Botanic Garden, and the nearby branch of the University of California have made the city a center for the study of natural history, and attracted nature-loving residents from all over the country and the world.

The Audubon emblem, the common egret, is a reminder that the national society was founded to save that bird from extinction. Similarly, the Santa Barbara Audubon Society has a special interest in preserving the California condor. It is not too much to say that in Southern California that great threatened bird is a symbol of survival, and of warning. The condor is our canary in the mine—the mine slowly filling with pollutants which is a possible image of our world—and if the condor survives, perhaps we may too.

This was one of the central ideas of a book about the condor which Bob Easton wrote with Dick Smith in the mid-1960s. This slim book marked a milestone.

The issue was not only the survival of the condor, but the preservation of the wilderness over which the condor flew. Both were threatened by Forest Service plans to build a paved road along the Sierra Madre Ridge, which marks the northern rim of the Sisquoc wilderness and is itself part of the condor flyway. The Sierra Madre Ridge road was put to sleep, only to be replaced by a larger but related issue.

This was the establishment of the San Rafael Wilderness Area, the first under the Wilderness Act of 1964. In its final dimensions, this national wilderness covers some 140,000 acres in the Santa Barbara back country. After many months of educational and political activity, activists went to Washington to see the expanded wilderness bill through Congress. They came back proud, feeling that Santa Barbara had established itself as a center of conservation in the west. This wilderness campaign helped to determine the strategy and tactics of the massive and continuing campaign against oil in our channel.

Santa Barbara had had to fight continually to preserve both her amenities and her reputation as a conservation center. Like most other Southern California cities, it had more than doubled in size since the war. It was faced with serious traffic problems and accompanying air and noise pollution. The overhead freeway proposed by the State Highway Division threatened to broadcast this pollution further, and to cut the downtown business section in two. Visible decay in the central part of the city called for rehabilitation and restoration.

The city resisted many threats. The wild growth that overran San Jose and other cities in this period was checked in Santa Barbara by the city's refusal to accept any but smokeless industry. The overhead freeway had been stalled for years, and plans for it are being gradually and reluctantly altered by the Highway Division. An enlightened citizen force led by Miss Pearl Chase prevented the building of high-rise apartments in the city, and has held back a later plan which would lead to suburban sprawl.

It was an ecologically aware citizen force that held the city together during the oil crisis. Though the city is quite conservative politically, and backed Nixon and Reagan in recent elections, it is far from devoid of intellectual activism. This activism can be reminiscent of a New England town meeting, where citizens are a functioning and vocal part of government. The civic life of Santa Barbara has been punctuated, loudly, by such meetings.

The oil crisis crept up on us in near silence. Concentrating on protecting the city and the surrounding lands, we didn't fully realize that the sea could be in danger. In my early years in Santa Barbara, I had made the narrator of a novel say: "I turned on my back and floated, looking up at the sky, nothing around me but cool clear Pacific, nothing in my eyes but long blue space. It was as close as I ever got to cleanliness and freedom, as far as I ever got from all the people. They had jerrybuilt the beaches from San Diego to the Golden Gate, bulldozed super-highways through the mountains, cut down a thousand years of redwood growth, and built an urban wilderness in the desert. They couldn't touch the ocean. They poured their sewage into it, but it couldn't be tainted."

My narrator and I were wrong. A series of oil drilling plat-forms had been erected in the state tidelands southeast of Santa Barbara. Now there was pressure for further platforms in the deeper and more treacherous federal waters outside the three-mile limit. The pressure was intensified by the federal government's need for money to finance the war in Indochina, and local government was unable to withstand it. A number of citizens tried to open public discussion on the matter, but the decision had already been made in Washington, based on In-terior Department findings which were rather loosely related to local reality. Without a public hearing, or any serious examination of the dangers of deep-water drilling in the earth-quake-prone channel, oil rights in large sections of the channel were auctioned off to the oil companies. After the damage was done, we learned why there had been no public hearings: a permanent official in the Interior Department had vetoed it on the grounds that it might "stir up the natives."

The great oil spill that began on January 28, 1969, failed to interrupt my beach walks, but it displaced other topics of conversation. I remember a day, about two weeks after the eruption, when I stopped on Mountain Drive and looked out over the contaminated sea. The flowing oil had been partly choked off, but it was still leaking up through the ruptured sea floor. Thousands of diving birds had died, and the quality of human life in the area was being threatened. The beaches were black for forty miles along the coast, and reblackened every day as the tides came in. The odor of crude oil reached me like the whiff of a decaying future.

It seemed that if the spill was to have a meaning, that mean-ing would have to be created by the men on the scene. Some-how the black disaster of Santa Barbara must be converted into a turning point in our history, a signpost marking the end of such ruinous environmental carelessness. This view was presented in an article for the *New York Times Magazine* which Bob Easton and I collaborated on.

We all shared the months of conflict and doubt, as it became clear that the lessons of the spill were being lost on the federal government and its favored industry, and that the sellout of the Santa Barbara Channel would be allowed to proceed. Slowly we realized that our fate was in our own hands, that only the people on the spot could hope to counter and change a self-destructive national policy. Citizen movements like GOO (Get Oil Out!) were organized, without whose advice and dissent both big government and big industry seem to be one-eyed giants. Citizen-litigants are still seeking in the federal courts a full disclosure from the government of the uncertain physical situation in the channel.

The issue, in Santa Barbara, is whether the environment can be bought and sold over citizens' objections, or whether there is an inalienable right to the use and enjoyment of air and water. It is a test case, between a pervasive new form of tyranny and an ancient freedom, which will help to determine the future conditions of life throughout the United States.

15

An Interview with
Ross Macdonald
by Ralph B. Sipper

INTERVIEWER: There is an implicit suggestion in your books that the detective novel is or should be changing so that it depicts society as it changes. Is this a valid interpretation?

MACDONALD: It is. My own books have changed a great deal over the past twenty-five years as society has changed. I'm trying to write about contemporary life and that is a moving target.

INTERVIEWER: One reviewer has said that you use the detective novel to explore the American psyche. Is this true?

MACDONALD: Well, I'm not sure I'd put it that way, exactly. What a writer explores is life as he knows it, the people he knows and himself. If his exploration is honest and far-reaching enough and if the material that he grasps at is relevant to the experience of his time, then he could be said to be exploring the American psyche. I won't deny that that's the sort of thing I'm interested in doing. Isn't that what every serious writer is trying to do? To explore the deepest feelings and thoughts of his time through representative characters.

INTERVIEWER: Certainly, but you seem to peer down into the subterranean layers more than most writers.

MACDONALD: I do try to, of course. But then, I'm psychologically oriented. I have been all of my life. And I've devised plot structures which reflect this.

INTERVIEWER: And you're also concerned with character, aren't you?

MACDONALD: Yes, I am. The individual human being is what interests me most. The only things that interest me more are the interactions and relationships between individual human beings: family and community and their ruptures.

INTERVIEWER: In connection with that, another reviewer has said that Chandler was more interested in the individual scenes as opposed to their sum, whereas for you, the entire plot structure is what counts.

MACDONALD: That's true. Chandler considered the scene to be the essential unit of fiction. He said that it was a good plot if it produced good scenes. I disagree. I think that the overall intention of a book is very much more important than the individual scenes, and the individual scenes have to reflect that intention. In other words, I believe in the principle of narrative unity.

INTERVIEWER: Lew Archer seems to differ from other fictional private eyes in that he elicits quite a bit of voluntary information from the people he is questioning. Why do they respond so willingly?

MACDONALD: Most people are eager to tell the truth about themselves, and any stranger can elicit a life story from them just by being interested.

INTERVIEWER: But don't people sometimes tell Archer things they later regret having revealed?

MACDONALD: Yes, they do. But you must understand that Archer, as he appears in my books, is always working in a crisis. Such a situation impels people to speak more freely.

INTERVIEWER: I would assume that you have known actual private eyes.

MACDONALD: Yes, I have known several. To give you an idea of what an actual private eye thinks of Archer's methods—I was visited some time ago by a successful private detective who had the thought that he and I might collaborate on a code of ethics for California private eyes. Perhaps he recognized in my fictional private eye the kind of *modus operandi* and ethical approach that he himself tried to practice.

INTERVIEWER: Although six of your earlier books did not have Archer as their narrator, you have stuck with him now in your last nine or ten books.

MACDONALD: Yes, I seem to do better with Archer. The form in general, and Archer in particular, seem to fulfill my needs as a writer and enable me to get into the material that I want to write about. When that ceases to be the case, I'll cast around for something else. I admit that it is a bit unusual for a writer of serious intentions to write so many books using the same central character. But, you know, there is a sense in which Archer is not the main character at all. He is, essentially, the observer and narrator. He is not the person that everything happens to. He observes what happens to my central figures, who are always changing.

INTERVIEWER: From the statistical point of view, a disproportionate number of murderers in your books turn out to be women. Why is this?

MACDONALD: Well, the truth is I don't base my books on statistics.

INTERVIEWER: I'm certain you don't, but why is it so often that a woman turns out to be the murderer?

MACDONALD: Perhaps because, in our society, I regard women as having, essentially, been victimized. In nearly every case the women in my books who commit murders have been victims. People who have been victims tend to victimize. There is a clear illustration of this in one of my breakthrough novels (as I like to think of them), *The Doomsters*.

INTERVIEWER: What makes a murderer?

MACDONALD: I think a murderer is someone who has been very severely injured, morally and emotionally. A murderer is someone who, so to speak, has himself been murdered to the point where he strikes back blindly and self-destructively. I am not speaking of professional killers. The average murderer in the United States is a man or woman who kills somebody he knows. Often, it is his wife or husband, or some member of the family, or someone close to the family. It is very often done on the spur of the moment under the influence of severe stress. I try to write about the domestic circumstances that might produce this kind of situation.

INTERVIEWER: For the past fifteen years or so, starting with *The Doomsters* or *The Galton Case,* you have been working with themes such as the search for the lost father, and the sins of the parents being visited upon the children. These are powerful themes uncommon to detective novels. Why do you deal with them?

MACDONALD: Most writers who produce an extensive body of work do so as a result of obsessions that they have. You have named two of mine. As we grow older the meanings of our obsessions gradually change, and mature as we mature. Some of the pain goes out of them and understanding enters, perhaps. So, we return to our obsessions and we reshape them. We reshape ourselves as we write.

INTERVIEWER: At one point you said, and I paraphrase, "You have to keep saying it (what you know) over and over again, getting closer each time to what is true." How close are you?

MACDONALD: The purpose of my kind of art is only to get close. The meaning is in the process. Writing is an organic process like breathing or eating. It has to feed the writer as he is writing or it won't feed other people. It has to be a living act which you do for your own sake in your own time. You don't just do it to produce a book. You do it to struggle with demons, to get them under control. I say demons, but I mean problems, memories, or whatever else makes up one's psychic life. To put it another way, you're wrestling with your own angels.

INTERVIEWER: How do you go about writing a book? That is, from conception to conclusion?

MACDONALD: Well, invariably, I start a book with an idea and it is, generally, a plot idea. For example, the original plot idea for *The Galton Case* was that Oedipus was angry at his parents for sending him away into a foreign country. That was why he killed his father. Now this was not in the Sophoclean or mythic version. It is what might be called a Freudian dramatization of the myth, but it's my own. It comes out of my own experience. Of course, this is not exactly what happens in the book. Ideas change by the time you get them into a book. You start with an idea. I do, anyway. Then you examine its developments and you start working out characters who can embody those developments, and events which show the characters developing over a period of years. I like plots which extend over a period of two or three generations so that I can show the whole apparatus of family influence or the lack ot if.

INTERVIEWER: How much time do you spend on a book?

MACDONALD: I spend from three to six months or even longer working out in notebooks various possible developments of my initial idea, story developments not written out as stories but

90

as synopses of possible events. I prepare life histories for my characters and I write them down so I don't forget them. At the end of six months I might decide not do do that book now but to wait for a while. Sometimes I wait as long as ten years. I very seldom write a book I've just initiated the planning of. I had been working on *Sleeping Beauty* for ten years before I finally finished it. In the meantime, however, I wrote other books. When I get ready actually to write a book I sit down with about three of my main ideas and with all the notebooks I've filled with them. Then I study the ideas, add to them, analyze them and then decide which one is right for me to do now, which one is going to incorporate the things I want to talk about this time. I try to get as much into a book as there is to be gotten into it. I try to follow out the meanings and the intentions of the book. That takes time. The actual writing of the book might take as long as nine months.

INTERVIEWER: The length of a pregnancy?

MACDONALD: You might say that. The actual writing of the book might take nine months, but behind that there might be nine years.

INTERVIEWER: So you let your ideas age like a bottle of wine?

MACDONALD: Not really, because nothing happens to the bottle of wine. I think about my books constantly, the way other people think about, perhaps, their friends and relatives. I think about the people in my books. They keep coming back to me.

INTERVIEWER: I can see why it takes time to do it that way.

MACDONALD: One of the two things a novelist needs is a lot of time. The other thing he needs is the willingness to sit in a room by himself during that time. I sit with my notebooks. These are the working habits of a scholar, really. I write a novel the way I wrote a dissertation. I do scholarship in the life of the present. You might call it the archaeology of the recent past.

INTERVIEWER: You have extended the use of imagery far beyond that of other writers of detective novels. With each succeeding book your images integrate more with your characters and themes. To what end?

MACDONALD: I think I am one of the few American detective story writers who have been fortunate enough to be able to learn from the poets how to handle imagery. Imagery is an essential feature of my writing and, as I've said before, I think I've managed to get some symbolic depth into it. I'm not just interested in a simile for the sake of what it does in the sentence. I'm interested in what it does in terms of the whole book. Some of my similes, I think, carry the message of my book better than anything else I write. For example, on page 3 of my latest book, *Sleeping Beauty*, I have written: "The wind had changed and I began to smell the floating oil. It smelled like something that had died but would never go away." Now on the surface this merely describes how the oil in the oil spill at the beginning of the book smelled. Actually, what I have done is to relate the floating oil to the whole background of death and criminal history in my book. "Something that had died but would never go away," is the tragic background of the Lennox family. I'm using my simile to incorporate the floating oil with the past so that one becomes representative of the other. The oil, then, becomes symbolic of the whole history of the Lennox family and its moral meaning, which is the intention of the book—to make a California oil spill a physical representative of the moral life of the people who caused it.

INTERVIEWER: And that's not easy to do, is it?

MACDONALD: It takes an entire book to do it completely. Imagery is a structural element. For me, it is almost the essential element.

INTERVIEWER: You have said of the hard-boiled detective novel that, "Its distinctive ingredient is a style which tries to catch the rhythms and some of the words of the spoken language." Later, in writing about Dashiell Hammett and Raymond Chandler, you said, "Their style, terse and highly figured, seemed not quite to have reached the end of its development." Do you think that you are reaching that end?

MACDONALD: No, I don't think I'm the terminal point of the hard-boiled detective story. In fact, there are a lot of young writers carrying on in our vein right now. I do think that what I sought to accomplish, and perhaps to some extent have succeeded in doing, was to invest the imagery and the language that I inherited from Hammett and Chandler with a symbolic depth which actually belongs in the language. People speak in symbolic depth and I'm writing as I feel people really speak, expressing their deepest thoughts in a semi-unspoken way.

INTERVIEWER: What trends do you see the detective novel taking in the future?

MACDONALD: I don't see any reason why it shouldn't spread out into a form of the general novel; that is, return to its origins. I've been trying to push it in that direction. I've been trying to put into my books the same sorts of things that a reader finds in the general novel, a whole version of life in our society and in our time. Of course, my books are somewhat limited by the kind of structure and subject matter that is inherent in the contemporary detective novel. I seem to work best within such limitations. The limitations of popular art can be liberating, as the history of the drama has often shown.

INTERVIEWER: Would you like to guess at the future of the detective novel?

MACDONALD: I don't know what it will be. It depends on the kind of writers it will attract. It seems to be attracting increasingly good ones. In the twenties there was just the one Hammett and a few good writers like Paul Cain. Nowadays, there are a great many highly competent writers involved in the writing of crime fiction. So I'm optimistic about the detective novel's future.

16

Great Stories of Suspense

T ALES OF TERROR and tabu were doubtless told in the firelit caves of our remotest ancestors. Though we pride ourselves on our modern rationality, we still seem to take a peculiar pleasure in the imaginative experience of frightful happenings. Perhaps, like Mithridates sampling his daily poison, we swallow our regular quotas of fictitious fear and danger in order to strengthen our minds against the real thing. Perhaps we need to be reminded that our planet is an uncertain and unsafe place, never completely controlled by the web of civilization that we have spun. Perhaps we like to play dangerous games without risk.

The discovery of startling facts and frightening truths seems to be the central feature of most stories of detection and suspense. The pure detective story is primarily concerned with what has happened, and moves backwards through time in search of an explanation. The pure suspense story is concerned with what is going to happen, and moves forward, often towards catastrophe. Most contemporary crime fiction tends to combine the elements of detection and suspense.

These stories develop a growing sense of discrepancy, of something wrong which may lead to something worse. In most pure detective stories, the very worst is averted through the efforts of the principal character, and evil is quelled and punished. But in stories of suspense the worst often occurs, and its fearful truth lights up the world of the story like nocturnal lightning. It may remind us that the world is still largely unknown, not wholly different from the world on which our ancestors looked out through their cave mouths. It may suggest that our own minds have secret places where the dangerous past still lies hidden.

The detective story offers some comfort against the dark, by showing that human reason may be a match for the antihuman forces in the world. In the usual tale of detection the crime of murder is allowed to occur, but the criminal is finally brought to justice. Tales of suspense are often less reassuring. Stanley Ellin's "The Payoff" and John Collier's "Wet Saturday" take away our breath and with it any hope that all will come right in the end. But they exhilarate the mind, teaching us how to deal with the cold fears and the hot impulses that plague us, and redrawing the ancient lines between good and evil.

Readers of crime fiction have long been divided into two main camps. Traditionalists tend to feel that the story of scientific detection is the true original form, and that everything since has been a falling-away. "Detection is, or ought to be, an exact science," as Sherlock Holmes once said to Dr. Watson, "and should be treated in the same cold and unemotional manner. To tinge it with romanticism produces much the same effect as if you worked a love-story or an elopement into the fifth proposition of Euclid." But other readers consider Holmes himself a rather romanticized figure whose cases sometimes fail to come to grips with reality. The contemporary English crime novelist and critic Julian Symons argues for a more serious use of the crime story: "Its author's business will always be to investigate, with all the freedom that the medium permits him, the springs of violence."

But though I rejoice in Mr. Symons's resolve to take the crime story seriously, I feel that the terms of that seriousness are too narrowly stated. To restrict it to the investigation of "the springs of violence" falls into the scientist fallacy, just as Sherlock Holmes's prescription does. Crime fiction is more imaginative than scientific (and this is certainly true of Julian Symons's novels). It is a free form of popular art, and like any other popular art it exists to be enjoyed. Its value lies first in its style and strength as a story, then in its revelation of the shapes and meanings of life in all their subtlety and surprise. It obeys the laws of narrative, which are not derived from either the chemist's laboratory or the psychologist's Rorschach test.

The Gothic novel was invented in what we nostalgically call the Age of Enlightenment. One of its foremost practitioners at the end of the eighteenth century was the English novelist Ann Radcliffe. A contemporary reviewer of her *Mysteries of Udolpho* (1794) explains her art as a sophisticated combination of the frightening and the reassuring: "Mysterious terrors are continually exciting in the mind the idea of a supernatural appearance . . . and yet are ingeniously explained by familiar causes; curiosity is kept upon the stretch from page to page."

The author of this review was the poet Coleridge, who in his later poem *Christabel* attempted a Gothic narrative in verse. But Coleridge was unable to finish *Christabel*. It was his American disciple Poe who, a generation later, took hold of the Gothic tradition and remolded it into its major modern forms— the tale of terror and suspense and the detective story.

Poe converted the short tale of terror into an art form which, like his poems, was a personal expression. As D.H. Lawrence wrote in the finest essay ever done on Poe, he was "an adventurer into vaults and cellars and horrible underground passages of the human soul. He sounded the horror and warning of his own doom." We can still use the heritage of guilty knowledge which Poe gave us in his wonderfully various tales. They were and are the foundation of modern suspense fiction in English.

Out of them grew Poe's second major invention in prose fiction, the detective story. I believe he invented it as a means of getting under control the terrible emotional and imaginative dislocations revealed in his tales of horror. His first and most famous detective story, "The Murders in the Rue Morgue," dwells like Mrs. Radcliffe's novels on weird and frightening events which are rationally explained. But the central fact to be accounted for—the body of a girl thrust up a chimney—has a realistic and symbolic force, and the explanation a logical complexity, which together seem peculiarly modern.

One reason for this may be that both Poe's explanation and the detective who provides it, M. Dupin, have been endlessly imitated by later writers. Dupin is a brilliant eccentric whom we see through the eyes of a somewhat less brilliant friend. The two most striking features of his investigative method, his quasi-scientific reliance on physical fact and his apparent ability to read minds by following the association of ideas, were taken up by Conan Doyle and given to Sherlock Holmes.

The line of descent from Poe's Dupin to Sherlock Holmes was not quite direct. Twenty years before Conan Doyle invented his famous character, Wilkie Collins had introduced into his novel *The Moonstone* (1868) an investigator based on an actual English detective, Inspector Whicher of the Constance Kent murder case. Even earlier, in 1860, Collins had produced in *The Woman in White* the first great modern mystery novel. This partly autobiographical "novel of sensation," as it was called, took a dark and knowing look at Victorian society, and particularly at its use and abuse of women.

Collins's great friend Dickens worked rather similar themes into his final novel. *The Mystery of Edwin Drood* (1870) dramatized Victorian England's social and moral schizophrenia in the double life of its central character. He is a cathedral choirmaster who becomes an opium user and possibly the murderer of his nephew Edwin. Though the mystery of the missing Edwin Drood remained unfinished and unsolved at Dickens's death, it leaves an overwhelming impression of a hypocritical society turning its back on it own lower depths, the drug-ridden, prostitute-haunted slums of London.

An even darker vision of Victorian London appears in *The Strange Case of Dr. Jekyll and Mr. Hyde*, which was written some sixteen years after *Edwin Drood* and was probably influenced by it. Though not in the modern sense a work of realism, it is a remarkably explicit and gripping account of a soul being lost by slow degrees and with its own complicity. As the double-minded villain-hero is drawn down through the gradations of crime and despair, the dualisms of the Victorian age are revealed and strangely resolved. The reader is transported to the night streets of a London where a short time later Jack the Ripper roamed and where, a short time after that, Sherlock Holmes and Dr. Watson set off by hansom cab on their errands of justice and mercy.

This late-Victorian hero Holmes, in spite of his scientific and ethical bent, was somewhat restless and ill at ease in his society. He fell prey to black bachelor moods. He played his violin to calm his nerves and, when the fit was on him, took hard drugs. Maurice Richardson has aptly described him as "a *fin-de-siècle* dropout" who later became a member of the establishment. For Holmes was a defender of the status quo, and in this respect Doyle's stories came to represent a falling-away from the deeper, questioning visions of Collins and Dickens. His final message is quietistic: England is safe in the hands of its ruling classes, and anyone who doubts this is a bounder, or possibly a nihilist.

This kind of social and psychological reassurance became a central feature of both the English and the American detective story in what was called, rather hopefully, its Golden Age. It became a formal game, played by rules that were derived from Poe and the Holmes canon rather than from the changing patterns of life. Its world of long weekends in country houses threatened to.become as artificial as the medieval courts of love. Even such formidable talents as Dorothy L. Sayers and S. S. Van Dine were sometimes betrayed into self-parody by fantasies of an unreal past and present. Agatha Christie invented in the twenties and developed in the thirties her light, strong tragicomic realism. But it was not until after the Second World War that she did her finest work, represented by the brilliant and humane novel about what Mrs. McGillicuddy and her friend Miss Marple saw.

The First World War and the social changes that followed it had already effected changes in the detective story. The passage from its Golden Age to its Age of Iron started in the United States in the twenties, with what might be called the *Black Mask* revolution. This crime magazine, edited at one time by H. L. Mencken and later by Joseph T. Shaw, encouraged a group of new writers to tell stories about the underworlds of such American cities as New York, San Francisco, Los Angeles, and Miami. Shaw was a demanding editor who enforced on his contributors a swift colloquial style. It was partly inspired by Hemingway's early stories, but also by the discovery by other writers of rich resources in the spoken language. The names of some of these writers were Lester Dent, Paul Cain, George Harmon Coxe, Raymond Chandler, and Dashiell Hammett.

Hammett became their leader, and the most potent imaginative force in the creation of the modern American detective story. His "Continental Op" stories (the finest of which is "Fly

Paper") expanded the social and moral range of the form, and set it talking in a prose which could say almost anything but often chose not to. The Continental Op's essential decency and courage are underplayed, and commonly shown in action, not in talk. Hammett's mature work, particularly in his two great novels *The Glass Key* and *The Maltese Falcon*, has a muted masculine force and a deadpan sincerity which together form a kind of tragic mask.

Though Sam Spade's adventures in *The Maltese Falcon* were based to some extent on Hammett's experiences as a private detective in San Francisco ("I was once falsely accused of perjury and had to perjure myself to escape arrest.") Hammett could see his hero from the outside, without vainglory or romanticism. This marks a sharp break with The Golden Age tradition of the detective as aristocratic superman. Spade is wholly committed to his difficult life, caught in the urban jungle, unable to rise above its tribal customs. He plays for the highest stakes available, a woman he seems to love and a jeweled bird he covets, and loses both. All he holds on to at the end is an obdurate male pride which is more Luciferian than Christian.

Raymond Chandler, who dedicated an early book to Hammett, softened and refined the powerful colloquial mechanisms of Hammett's prose and used it to celebrate a more perfect gentle knight, in the person of Marlowe. The influence of these two writers enlarged the detective story and spread far beyond it, to leave a permanent mark on modern fiction in general. I learned my craft from them, and from their contemporary James M. Cain.

Cain, whose father was an eastern college president and whose mother was an opera singer, grounded his work in the common language and the people who spoke it. He once confessed that he was unable to write convincing fiction until he heard a western rough-neck talk. One of the happy consequences was "The Baby in the Icebox." This uproarious story about an escaped tiger walks a difficult and daring line between farce and melodrama. It is humanized by the voice of its narrator, an illiterate man who is capable of honesty and love.

There were parallel and related developments in England, where Graham Greene had begun to use his crime novels to hold a whole society up to view. Greene's serious interest in the inner life of his characters made the superficial elegances of the Golden Age look like peeling gilt. *This Gun for Hire* and *Brighton Rock* were ruthless in the portraiture of their villain-heroes, yet at the same time concerned with the salvation of their souls. *The Confidential Agent*, a beautifully constructed novel about terrible things, shows us a decent man going down to defeat in a lapsed world where the Second World War was being prepared.

The most profoundly moving of Greene's short stories, "The Basement Room" recounts a small boy's introduction to fear and loss. It is illuminated tragically by the author's daring forward-flashes into the later life of the man whom the frightened little boy eventually became. Through Greene's work, English crime literature began to regain its conscience, social and otherwise. It became aware of contemporary movements in psychiatry and anthropology and religion. Without losing its compulsive power to fascinate and thrill—indeed it gained in this power as it became more searching—the story of mystery and crime became a branch of the modern English novel.

One of the most valuable contributions made by those great trail-blazers Greene and Hammett was the gift of freedom they offered to other writers by their example. Without it, our leading contemporary writers might never have dared the bold originality of their mature work. We might never have had Julian Symons's uncompromising explorations of the roots of crime, or Patricia Highsmith's brilliant tragicomic plots stitching together the fragments of an amoral society. Even a wholly different writer like the exuberantly masculine Dick Francis belongs in the same line of descent, perhaps as close to Hammett as to Greene.

Francis was a leading jockey, indeed he had been the Queen's Jockey, before he took up writing a dozen or so years ago. Most of his novels have to do with horse racing and are full of movement, but running through their leaping action is a realistic understanding of the whole range of English life. *Enquiry*, in the course of telling a breathless story about a jockey robbed of his right to ride, takes a hard look at the English class system and its residual cruelties, from the point of view of a narrator-hero who had started at the bottom and worked his way up. In the works of such writers as these, the transatlantic mystery novel is reaching back towards the strength and depth that Dickens and Wilkie Collins gave it at the start.

Developments in the American mystery field have been equally various and interesting. In 1941, Howard Haycraft had already noticed the abandonment of "rigid formulas in favor of blending the detective elements with the novel of manners and character." The realistic vein opened up by the *Black Mask* writers was enriched by the influence of the ancient classics and modern psychoanalysis. Some of the most original and elegant work to come out of this new meld was done by Margaret Millar and by Kenneth Fearing.

Fearing was a recognized poet who wrote only two suspense novels. The better of these, *The Big Clock* (1941), is about a murder and a manhunt in a New York publishing empire. Narrated with force and speed and wit by several voices, it has lasting value as a record of metropolitan life, both outer and inner. In the nearly twenty years since it was written, its clean, brilliant style has shown no sign of fading. Its suspense still catches continually at the throat, and its jokes are still funny. Fearing's novel, which moves with love and knowledge through New York as G. K. Chesterton's stories moved through London, reminds me of Chesterton's description of the mystery story as "the earliest and only form of popular literature in which is expressed some sense of the poetry of modern life."

I hope these words may be applicable to my own stories. *The Far Side of the Dollar*, an account of an apparent kidnapping, moves through California and the Southwest towards an ending which attempts (as James M. Cain once said of one of his books) to "graze tragedy." The novel belongs not so much to my detective-narrator Archer as to the other people in the book. Archer is a man of action as well as an observer and recorder, but the emphasis is not on his physical exploits. He is less the hero of the novel than its mind, an unwilling judge who is forced to see that a murderer can be his own chief victim.

The present and the preceding generation of writers have

been marvelously rich in short suspense fiction which touches the central nerves of modern life. Patricia Highsmith's "The Terrapin" is a deeply realized account of unconscious cruelty and terrible retribution. The stories of those great stylists John Collier and Roald Dahl haunt our minds like memories of our most frightening and self-revealing dreams. Both "Wet Saturday" and "The Landlady" are brief masterpieces, written with the economy of poems. A leading American rival in the art of saying much in little, Stanley Ellin, has told us in the short compass of "The Payoff" nearly everything that we need to know about the irreparable human damage caused by war. Michael Gilbert's "The Amateur" is a story of comparable ferocity, which also notices the continuity between war and crime.

John Cheever and the late Flannery O'Connor are among the greatest American writers of their generation, and probably its two best short story writers. Cheever's "The Five-Forty-Eight" and O'Connor's "The Comforts of Home" are tragicomic stories of guilt and punishment which have the intensity of dramatic poetry, combined with the bite of reality. Each in its way is concerned with the destruction of a man through his attempt to destroy a woman. Indeed all of these stories are about the damage that we do to one another and urge us quietly to change our ways.

But aren't such stories literature rather than suspense fiction? I believe they belong in both categories. The Gothic tradition and the conventions of the crime story that grew out of it have always nourished both popular and serious literature. They are a medium of communication between the popular and the serious, making the former more meaningful, the latter more lively.

A strong popular convention like that of the suspense story is both an artistic and a social heritage. It keeps the forms of the art alive for the writer to use. It trains his readers, endowing both writer and reader with a common vocabulary of structural shapes and narrative possibilities. It becomes a part of the language in which we think and feel, reaching our whole society and helping to hold our civilization together.

Suspense fiction presents a view of modern life as dangerous and flawed but not beyond redemption, a vision in which almost any crime or disaster can be contained and understood. Somehow it helps to take the curse off trouble, perhaps because it is, for both writer and reader, an art form which is also a game of skill. In its highest reaches, where Flannery O'Connor and a few others work their miracles, the reader hardly knows whether to laugh or cry or cheer.

17

The Death
of the Detective

(World Crime Writers Conference, 1978)

M Y LOVE AFFAIR with the Gothic muse has passed through a number of stages, roughly matching the stages of my life. It started in silent movies where Pearl White repeatedly risked her neck in order to preserve her virginity. In my foolish adolescence I ruined my eyes and sharpened my taste on hundreds of mystery novels. Then in the euphoria of my later teens I read Coleridge's unfinished *Christabel* and conceived the intention of finishing it for him. Later I backed away from this wild ambition, and replaced it with a dissertation on Coleridge's philosophic origins. So much for Dr. Jekyll. At night as Mr. Hyde, I haunted the deserted rooms of Angell Hall in Ann Arbor, and began to write a spy story set in that same university building.

I failed to see until later in my life how these various levels of dreaming were related to each other. But through all of them I was preparing myself to become what for convenience' sake I will call a Gothic novelist. That excellent Gothic novelist Mrs. Radcliffe had been given more than one favorable review by Coleridge when he was at the height of his youthful powers. His unfinished poem *Christabel* was in effect a Gothic novel in verse. And it was Coleridge's disciple Edgar Allan Poe who invented the modern detective story, laying out a basic pattern which persisted through the works of Conan Doyle, Dorothy L. Sayers, and even the late Rex Stout. I am citing these historical connections not so much to claim relationship with great

105

names as to suggest that our Gothic forms, which we have gathered here to celebrate and criticize this week, support a vast literary movement which has persisted now for nearly two centuries, and is going stronger than ever.

The early Gothic writers learned in its modern sense the fear of death, and were deeply involved with the question—the Frankenstein question—whether man was a spirit or an animal. (Or which came over first, the chicken or the ego?) Natural science was stating the case for the animal in increasingly strong terms. The controlled spiritual life which had traditionally nourished the arts was threatened by more immediate knowledge, and experiences psychological and naturalistic. Such knowledge and its consequences were imagined in detail by Coleridge in *The Ancient Mariner*, which was a Fall of Man in miniature, by Coleridge's disciple Poe in his poems and stories, and by well over a century of English and American detective fiction.

I think the urge toward literary detection must arise from a need for meaning in lives which have been stripped of some prior meaning. The solution of a crime like murder seems to reinject into our lives a saving grace, a more humane and tragic knowledge. Still the separate halves of this divided world, mind and matter, spirit and flesh, seem to be rather mechanically related. We and our detectives know spirit and flesh only in their separateness, as clues to each other. But the truth that the clues should lead us to is already in the past: the death of a world, or the death of the one of its creatures. We sit with our backs to the future unsnarling our tangled lines and the damaged symbols they have dragged up from the depths. In the new Gothic imaginary world the mind is trapped by an irreversible event: it has fallen.

And in the psychological life, where a beleaguered remnant of the spiritual holds on, there are painful movements which cannot easily be reversed. The murder story is epic or gospel without those forms' saving grandeurs or graces—a story which recreates at some great distance the fall of man, his death, and his survival. Such fiction offers the mind some knowledge and control, but tends to return that knowledge to the physical, the scientific, the social, the merely commensurable. The center of man is usually avoided as if there were a

106

darkness there, beyond the reach of understanding.

Such figures as Spade and Marlowe and more recently Laidlaw and others have brought some tragic feeling back into the mystery novel. But in the works of Hammett and Chandler there is a persistent division between the hunter and the hunted, the knower and the known, which suppresses this feeling to some extent. There can be no moral safety in the fully tragic world.

The detective may grow old and eventually does, but in the meantime he is invulnerable, perhaps miserable but invulnerable. He deals in death but is untouched by it. Perhaps in his essence he represents our lingering fear of death, and our consequent inability to submit ourselves or our imaginations to tragic life. We live in the illusion of the hunter even while we are being hunted.

18

Homage to
Dashiell Hammett

I HAVE BEEN GIVEN some space to speak for the hardboiled school of mystery writing. Let me use it to dwell for a bit on the work of Dashiell Hammett. He was the great innovator who invented the hardboiled detective novel and used it to express and master the undercurrent of inchoate violence that runs through so much of American life.

In certain ways, it must be admitted, Hammett's heroes are reminiscent of unreconstructed Darwinian man; *McTeague* and *The Sea Wolf* stand directly behind them. But no matter how rough and appetent they may be, true representatives of a rough and appetent society, they are never allowed to run unbridled. Hammett's irony controls them. In fact he criticized them far more astringently and basically than similar men were criticized by Hemingway. In his later and less romantic moments Hammett was a close and disillusioned critic of the two-fisted hard-drinking woman-chasing American male that he derived partly from tradition and partly from observation, including self-observation.

Even in one of his very early stories, first published by Mencken in *Smart Set,* Hammett presents a character who might have been a parody of the Hemingway hero, except that he was pre-Hemingway. This huge brute is much attached to his beard. To make a short story shorter, the loss of his beard reveals that he used it to hide a receding chin and make him a public laughingstock. This isn't much more than an anecdote, but it suggests Hammett's attitude towards the half-evolved frontier male of our not too distant past. Shorn and urbanized, he became in Hammett's best novels a near-tragic figure, a lonely and suspicious alien who pits a hopeless but obstinate animal courage against the metropolitan jungle, a not very moral man who clings with a skeptic's desperation to a code of behavior empirically arrived at in a twilight world between chivalry and gangsterism.

Like the relationship of Charles Dickens and Wilkie Collins, the Hemingway-Hammett influence ran two ways. Hammett achieved some things that Hemingway never attempted. He placed his characters in situations as complex as those of life, in great cities like San Francisco and New York and Baltimore, and let them work out their dubious salvations under social and economic and political pressures. The subject of his novels, you might say, was the frontier male thrust suddenly, as the frontier disappeared, into the modern megalopolis; as Hemingway's was a similar man meeting war and women, and listening to the silence of his own soul.

Hammett's prose is not quite a prose that can say anything, as Chandler overenthusiastically claimed it could. But it is a clean useful prose, with remarkable range and force. It has pace and point, strong tactile values, the rhythms and colors of speech, all in the colloquial tradition that stretches from Mark Twain through Stephen Crane to Lardner and Mencken, the Dr. Johnson of our vernacular. Still it is a deadpan and rather external prose, artificial-seeming compared with Huck Finn's earthy rhetoric, flat in comparison with Fitzgerald's more subtly colloquial instrument. Hammett's ear for the current and the colloquial was a little too sardonically literal, and this is already tending to date his writing, though not seriously.

Analysis of any kind is alien to this prose. Moulding the surface of things, it lends itself to the vivid narration of rapid, startling action. Perhaps it tends to set too great a premium on action, as if the mind behind it were hurrying away from its own questions and deliberately restricting itself to the manipulation of appearances. It is in part the expression of that universally-met-with American type who avoids sensibility and introspection because they make you vulnerable in the world. At its worst such prose can be an unnecessary writing-down to the lowest common denominator of the democracy. But at its best it has great litotic power, as in some of Hemingway's earlier stories, or in the haunting chapter where Sam Spade makes devious love to Brigid by telling her the story of Flitcraft:

"A man named Flitcraft had left his real-estate office, in Tacoma, to go to luncheon one day and had never returned. He did not keep an engagement to play golf after four that afternoon, though he had taken the initiative in making the engagement less than half an hour before he went out to luncheon. His wife and children never saw him again. His wife and he were supposed to be on the best of terms. He had two children, boys, one five and the other three. He owned his house in a Tacoma suburb, a new Packard, and the rest of the appurtenances of successful American living."

Sam Spade is Flitcraft's spiritual twin, the lonely male who is not at ease in Zion or in Zenith. He is inarticulate about himself, like Babbitt is aware only of a deep malaise that spurs him on to action and acquisition. *The Maltese Falcon* is a fable of modern man in quest of love and money, despairing of everything else. Its murders are more or less incidental, though they help to give it its quality of a crisis novel. Its characters act out of the extreme emotions of fear and guilt and concupiscence, anger and revenge; and with such fidelity to these passions that their natures almost seem co-terminous with them.

Driven by each and all of them, Sam Spade strips away one by one the appearances which stand between him and the truth, and between him and the complete satisfaction of his desires. His story ends in drastic peripeteia with the all but complete frustration of his desires. His lover is guilty of murder; the code without which his life is meaningless forces him to turn her over to the police. The black bird is hollow. The reality behind appearances is a treacherous vacuum. Spade turns for sardonic consolation to the wife of his murdered partner (whose name was Archer). It is his final reluctant act of animal pragmatism.

Probably Hammett intended the ultimate worthlessness of the Maltese falcon to be more than a bad joke on his protagonist. I see it as the symbol of a lost tradition, representing the great cultures of the past which have become inaccessible to Spade and the men of his time. It represents explicitly the religious and ethical developments of the Mediterranean basin, Christianity and knight-errantry. Perhaps it stands for the Holy Ghost itself, or rather for its absence.

In any case the bird's lack of value implies Hammett's final comment on the inadequacy and superficiality of Sam Spade's life and ours. If only his bitterly inarticulate struggle for self-realization were itself more fully realized, the stakes for which he plays not so arbitrarily lost from the beginning (a basic limitation of the detective story is that its action is pre-ordained, in a sense, by what has already happened), Sam Spade could have been a great indigenous tragic figure. Maybe he is. I think *The Maltese Falcon*, with its astonishing imaginative energy persisting undiminished after a third of a century, is tragedy of a new kind, deadpan tragedy.

19

The Writer As Detective Hero

APRODUCER WHO LAST YEAR was toying with the idea of making a television series featuring my private detective Lew Archer asked me over lunch at Perino's if Archer was based on any actual person. "Yes," I said. "Myself." He gave me a semi-pitying Hollywood look. I tried to explain that while I had known some excellent detectives and watched them work, Archer was created from the inside out. I wasn't Archer, exactly, but Archer was me.

The conversation went downhill from there, as if I had made a damaging admission. But I believe most detective-story writers would give the same answer. A close paternal or fraternal relationship between writer and detective is a marked peculiarity of the form. Throughout its history, from Poe to Chandler and beyond, the detective hero has represented his creator and carried his values into action in society.

Poe, who invented the modern detective story, and his detective Dupin, are good examples. Poe's was a first-rate but guilt-haunted mind painfully at odds with the realities of pre-Civil-War America. Dupin is a declassed aristocrat, as Poe's heroes tend to be, an obvious equivalent for the artist-intellectual who has lost his place in society and his foothold in tradition. Dupin has no social life, only one friend. He is set apart from other people by his superiority of mind.

In his creation of Dupin, Poe was surely compensating for his failure to become what his extraordinary mental powers

113

seemed to fit him for. He had dreamed of an intellectual hierarchy governing the cultural life of the nation, himself at its head. Dupin's outwitting of an unscrupulous politician in "The Purloined Letter," his "solution" of an actual New York case in "Marie Roget," his repeated trumping of the cards held by the Prefect of Police, are Poe's vicarious demonstrations of superiority to an indifferent society and its officials.

Of course Poe's detective stories gave the writer, and give the reader, something deeper than such obvious satisfactions. He devised them as a means of exorcising or controlling guilt and horror. The late William Carlos Williams, in a profound essay, related Poe's sense of guilt and horror to the terrible awareness of a hyperconscious man standing naked and shivering on a new continent. The guilt was doubled by Poe's anguished insight into the unconscious mind. It had to be controlled by some rational pattern, and the detective story, "the tale of ratiocination," provided such a pattern.

The tale of the bloody murders in the "Rue Morgue," Poe's first detective story (1841), is a very hymn to analytic reason intended, as Poe wrote later, "to depict some very remarkable features in the mental character of my friend, the Chevalier C. Auguste Dupin." Dupin clearly represents the reason, which was Poe's mainstay against the nightmare forces of the mind. These latter are acted out by the murderous ape: "Gnashing its teeth, and flashing fire from is eyes, it flew upon the body of the girl and embedded its fearful talons in her throat, retaining its grasp until she expired."

Dupin's reason masters the ape and explains the inexplicable—the wrecked apartment behind the locked door, the corpse of a young woman thrust up the chimney—but not without leaving a residue of horror. The nightmare can't quite be explained away, and persists in the teeth of reason. An unstable balance between reason and more primitive human qualities is characteristic of the detective story. For both writer and reader it is an imaginative arena where such conflicts can be worked out safely, under artistic controls.

The first detective story has other archetypal features, particularly in the way it is told. The "I" who narrates it is not the detective Dupin. The splitting of the protagonist into a narrator and a detective has certain advantages: it helps to eliminate the

114

inessential, and to postpone the solution. More important, the author can present his self-hero, the detective, without undue embarrassment, and can handle dangerous emotional material at two or more removes from himself, as Poe does in "Rue Morgue."

The disadvantages of the split protagonist emerge more clearly in the saga of Dupin's successor Sherlock Holmes. One projection of the author, the narrator, is made to assume a posture of rather blind admiration before another projection of the author, the detective hero, and the reader is invited to share Dr. Watson's adoration of the great man. An element of narcissistic fantasy, impatient with the limits of the self, seems to be built into this traditional form of the detective story.

I'm not forgetting that Holmes' *modus operandi* was based on that of an actual man, Conan Doyle's friend and teacher, Dr. Joseph Bell. Although his "science" usually boils down to careful observation, which was Dr. Bell's forte, Holmes is very much the scientific criminologist. This hero of scientism may be in fact the dominant culture hero of our technological society.

Though Holmes is a physical scientist specializing in chemistry and anatomy, and Dupin went in for literary and psychological analysis, Holmes can easily be recognized as Dupin's direct descendant. His most conspicuous feature, his ability to read thoughts on the basis of associative clues, is a direct borrowing from Dupin. And like Dupin, he is a projection of the author, who at the time of Holmes' creation was a not very busy young doctor. According to his son Adrian, Conan Doyle admitted when he was dying: "If anyone is Sherlock Holmes, then I confess it is myself."

Holmes had other ancestors and collateral relations which reinforce the idea that he was a portrait of the artist as a great detective. His drugs, his secrecy and solitude, his moods of depression (which he shared with Dupin) are earmarks of the Romantic rebel then and now. Behind Holmes lurk the figures of nineteenth-century poets, Byron certainly, probably Baudelaire, who translated Poe and pressed Poe's guilty knowledge to new limits. I once made a case for the theory (and Anthony Boucher didn't disagree) that much of the modern development of the detective story stems from Baudelaire, his

115

"dandyism" and his vision of the city as inferno. Conan Doyle's London, which influenced Eliot's "Wasteland," has something of this quality.

But Holmes' Romantic excesses aren't central to his character. His Baudelairean spleen and drug addiction are merely the idiosyncrasies of genius. Holmes is given the best of both worlds, and remains an English gentleman, accepted on the highest social levels. Permeating the thought and language of Conan Doyle's stories is an air of blithe satisfaction with a social system based on privilege.

This obvious characteristic is worth mentioning because it was frozen into one branch of the form. Nostalgia for a privileged society accounts for one of the prime attractions of the traditional English detective story and its innumerable American counterparts. Neither wars nor the dissolution of governments and societies interrupt that long weekend in the country house which is often, with more or less unconscious symbolism, cut off by a failure in communications from the outside world.

The contemporary world is the special province of the American hardboiled detective story. Dashiell Hammett, Raymond Chandler, and the other writers for *Black Mask* who developed it, were in conscious reaction against the Anglo-American school which, in the work of S. S. Van Dine for example, had lost contact with contemporary life and language. Chandler's dedication, to the editor of *Black Mask*, of a collection of his early stories (1944), describes the kind of fiction they had been trying to supplant: "For Joseph Thompson Shaw with affection and respect, and in memory of the time when we were trying to get murder away from the upper classes, the weekend house party and the vicar's rose-garden, and back to the people who are really good at it." While Chandler's novels swarm with plutocrats as well as criminals, and even with what pass in Southern California for aristocrats, the *Black Mask* revolution was a real one. From it emerged a new kind of detective hero, the classless, restless man of American democracy, who spoke the language of the street.

Hammett, who created the most powerful of these new heroes in Sam Spade, had been a private detective and knew the corrupt inner workings of American cities. But Sam Spade was a less obvious projection of Hammett than detective heroes usually are of their authors. Hammett had got his early romanticism under strict ironic control. He could see Spade from outside, without affection, perhaps with some bleak compassion. In this as in other respects Spade marks a sharp break with the Holmes tradition. He possesses the virtues and follows the code of a frontier male. Thrust for his sins into the urban inferno, he pits his courage and cunning against its denizens, plays for the highest stakes available, love and money, and loses nearly everything in the end. His lover is guilty of murder; his narrow, bitter code forces Spade to turn her over to the police. The Maltese falcon has been stripped of jewels.

Perhaps the stakes and implied losses are higher than I have suggested. The worthless falcon may symbolize a lost tradition, the great cultures of the Mediterranean past which have become inaccessible to Spade and his generation. Perhaps the bird stands for the Holy Ghost itself, or for its absence.

The ferocious intensity of the work, the rigorous spelling-out of Sam Spade's deprivation of his full human heritage, seem to me to make his story tragedy, if there is such a thing as deadpan tragedy. Hammett was the first American writer to use the detective-story for the purposes of a major novelist, to present a vision, blazing if disenchanted, of our lives. Sam Spade was the product and reflection of a mind which was not at home in Zion or in Zenith.

Chandler's vision is disenchanted, too, but in spite of its hallucinated brilliance of detail it lacks the tragic unity of Hammett's. In his essay on "The Simple Art of Murder," an excitingly written piece of not very illuminating criticism, Chandler offers a prescription for the detective hero which suggests a central weakness in his vision:

> In everything that can be called art there is a quality of redemption . . . But down these mean streets a man must go who is not himself mean, who is neither tarnished nor afraid . . . The detective in this kind of story must be such a man. He is the hero, he is everything . . . He must be the best man in his world and a good enough man for any world.

While there may be "a quality of redemption" in a good novel, it belongs to the whole work and is not the private property of one of the characters. No hero of serious fiction could act within a moral straitjacket requiring him to be consistently virtuous and unafraid. Sam Spade was submerged and struggling in tragic life. The detective-as-redeemer is a backward step in the direction of sentimental romance, and an over-simplified world of good guys and bad guys. The people of Chandler's early novels, though they include chivalrous gangsters and gangsters' molls with hearts of gold, are divided into two groups by an angry puritanical morality. The goats are usually separated from the sheep by sexual promiscuity or perversion. Such a strong and overt moralistic bias actually interferes with the broader moral effects a novelist aims at.

Fortunately in the writing of his books Chandler toned down his Watsonian enthusiasm for his detective's moral superiority. The detective Marlowe, who tells his own stories in the first person, and sometimes admits to being afraid, has a self-deflating wit which takes the curse off his knight-errantry:

> I wasn't wearing a gun . . . I doubted if it would do me any good. The big man would probably take it away from me and eat it. (*Farewell, My Lovely*, 1940)

The Chandler-Marlowe prose is a highly charged blend of laconic wit and imagistic poetry set to breakneck rhythms. Its strong colloquial vein reaffirms the fact that the *Black Mask* revolution was a revolution in language as well as subject matter. It is worth noticing that H. L. Mencken, the great lexicographer of our vernacular, was an early editor of *Black Mask*. His protegé James M. Cain once said that his discovery of the western roughneck made it possible for him to write fiction. Marlowe and his predecessors performed a similar function for Chandler, whose English education put a special edge on his passion for our new language, and a special edge on his feelings against privilege. Socially mobile and essentially classless (he went to college but has a workingclass bias), Marlowe liberated his author's imagination into an overheard democratic prose which is one of the most effective narrative instruments in our recent literature.

Under the obligatory "tough" surface of the writing, Marlowe is interestingly different from the standard hardboiled hero who came out of *Black Mask*. Chandler's novels focus in his hero's sensibility, and could almost be described as novels of sensibility. Their constant theme is big-city loneliness, and the wry pain of a sensitive man coping with the roughest elements of a corrupt society.

It is Marlowe's doubleness that makes him interesting: the hard-boiled mask half-concealing Chandler's poetic and satiric mind. Part of our pleasure derives from the interplay between the mind of Chandler and the voice of Marlowe. The recognized difference between them is part of the dynamics of the narrative, setting up bipolar tensions in the prose. The marvellous opening paragraph of *The Big Sleep* (1939) will illustrate some of this:

> It was about eleven o'clock in the morning, mid October, with the sun not shining and a look of hard wet rain in the clearness of the foothills. I was wearing my powder-blue suit, with dark blue shirt, tie and display handkerchief, black brogues, black wool socks with dark blue clocks on them. I was neat, clean, shaved and sober, and I didn't care who knew it. I was everything the well-dressed private detective ought to be. I was calling on four million dollars.

Marlowe is making fun of himself, and of Chandler in the rôle of brash young detective. There is pathos, too, in the idea that a man who can write like a fallen angel should be a mere private eye; and Socratic irony. The gifted writer conceals himself behind Marlowe's cheerful mindlessness. At the same time the retiring, middle-aged, scholarly author acquires a durable mask, forever 38, which allows him to face the dangers of society high and low.

Chandler's conception of Marlowe, and his relationship with his character, deepened as his mind penetrated the romantic fantasy, and the overbright self-consciousness, that limited his vision. At the end of *The Long Goodbye* (1953) there is a significant confrontation between Marlowe and a friend who had betrayed him and apparently gone homosexual. In place of the righteous anger which Marlowe would have indulged in in one of the earlier novels he now feels grief and disquiet, as if the confrontation might be with a part of himself.

The friend, the ex-friend, tries to explain his moral breakdown: "I was in the commandos, bud. They don't take you if you're just a piece of fluff. I got badly hurt and it wasn't any fun with those Nazi doctors. It did something to me." This is all we are told. At the roaring heart of Chandler's maze there is a horror which even at the end of his least evasive novel remains unspeakable. Whatever its hidden meaning, this scene was written by a man of tender and romantic sensibility who had been injured. Chandler used Marlowe to shield while half-expressing his sensibility, and to act out of the mild paranoia which often goes with this kind of sensibility and its private hurts, and which seems to be virtually endemic among contemporary writers.

I can make this judgment with some assurance because it applies with a vengeance to some of my earlier books, particularly *Blue City* (1947). A decade later, in *The Doomsters*, I made my detective Archer criticize himself as "a slightly earthbound Tarzan in a slightly paranoid jungle." This novel marked a fairly clean break with the Chandler tradition, which it had taken me some years to digest, and freed me to make my own approach to the crimes and sorrows of life.

I learned a great deal from Chandler—any writer can—but there had always been basic differences between us. One was in our attitude to plot. Chandler described a good plot as one that made for good scenes, as if the parts were greater than the whole. I see plot as a vehicle of meaning. It should be as complex as contemporary life, but balanced enough to say true things about it. The surprise with which a detective novel concludes should set up tragic vibrations which run backward through the entire structure. Which means that the structure must be single, and *intended.*

Another difference between Chandler and me is in our use of language. My narrator Archer's wider and less rigidly stylized range of expression, at least in more recent novels, is related to a central difference between him and Marlowe. Marlowe's voice is limited by his rôle as the hardboiled hero. He must speak within his limits as a character, and these limits are quite narrowly conceived. Chandler tried to relax them in *The Long Goodbye*, but he was old and the language failed to respond. He was trapped like the late Hemingway in an unnecessarily limiting idea of self, hero, and language.

I could never write of Archer: "He is the hero, he is everything." It is true that his actions carry the story, his comments on it reflect my attitudes (but deeper attitudes remain implicit), and Archer or a narrator like him is indispensable to the kind of books I write. But he is not their emotional center. And in spite of what I said at the beginning, Archer has developed away from his early status as a fantasy projection of myself and my personal needs. Cool, I think, is the word for our mature relationship. Archer himself has what New Englanders call "weaned affections."

An author's heavy emotional investment in a narrator-hero can get in the way of the story and blur its meanings, as some of Chandler's books demonstrate. A less encumbered narrator permits greater flexibility, and fidelity to the intricate truths of life. I don't have to celebrate Archer's physical or sexual prowess, or work at making him consistently funny and charming. He can be self-forgetful, almost transparent at times, and concentrate as good detectives (and good writers) do, on the people whose problems he is investigating. These other people are for me the main thing: they are often more intimately related to me and my life than Lew Archer is. He is the obvious self-projection which holds the eye (my eye as well as the reader's) while more secret selves creep out of the woodwork behind the locked door. Remember how the reassuring presence of Dupin permitted Poe's mind to face the nightmare of the homicidal ape and the two dead women.

Archer is a hero who sometimes verges on being an anti-hero. While he is a man of action, his actions are largely directed to putting together the stories of other people's lives and discovering their significance. He is less a doer than a questioner, a consciousness in which the meanings of other lives emerge. This gradually developed conception of the detective hero as the mind of the novel is not wholly new, but it is probably my main contribution to this special branch of fiction. Some such refinement of the conception of the detective hero was needed to bring this kind of novel closer to the purpose and range of the mainstream novel.

It may be that internal realism, a quality of mind, is one of the most convincing attributes a character can have. Policemen and lawyers have surprised me with the opinion that Archer is quite true to life. The two best private detectives I personally know resemble him in their internal qualities: their intelligent humaneness, an interest in other people transcending their interest in themselves, and a toughness of mind which enables them to face human weaknesses, including their own, with open eyes. Both of them dearly love to tell a story.

20

F. Scott Fitzgerald

(from Kenneth Millar's notebooks)

I THINK WHEN FITZGERALD said that he was the last for a time, he may have had in mind the fact that he was the last writer to embody the national fate, the last who swallowed whole the vast Platonic hubris of the Romantics, (Gatsby is said to have 'drunk the Platonic milk of wonder'), the last who saw himself as a kind of dizzy philosopher-king at the apex of society, the last who projected his subjective life in fiction as a kind of tragic legend for his age and for future time. He suffered it out in his mind and ego—his personal self and his own fate central to all his fiction—and died as he wrote it.

Even in his short life—he died in 1940 aged 44—Fitzgerald had outlived his age and a new age had begun. The Platonic dream had withered in the depression, and what was left of romantic egoism died in the war. Writers ceased to appear as the central figures of their own novels: the inability of Norman Mailer, for instance, to project and sustain such a self-figure forced him eventually into the nonfiction novel, a contradiction in terms but a necessary one. A profoundly less facile writer like Nelson Algren went underground in both his life and his work. Abandoning the aristocracy of art, which is one of the lost illusions of the Romantics, Algren lived in Chicago among the dispossessed ethnics that he wrote about. Just as he submerged himself in life, he went underground in his work, cutting it free from the controlling emotional image that was central in Fitzgerald or in Hemingway. His people are profoundly imagined but unimaginative, deeply felt but felt

123

by an invisible author. There is no savior and no salvation. The poetry is in the pity, as Wilfred Owen said about his war poems. The forms of society and personality had dissolved and run together in new forms, and Algren's imagination followed them. The imaginative country of romantic writers from Byron and Poe to Fitzgerald is the kingdom or the duchy; that of Algren (or Hammett) is the city or the ward, inhabited by underground men.

The Three Roads (1948) my first California novel, took a big step into the darkness. Its central character Bret was a member of the establishment, a mature officer in the U.S. Naval Reserve (as I had been). But if he is a hero at all, he is a seriously flawed one. As the novel opens he is a patient on the mental ward of the San Diego naval hospital, trying to remember his own past. His past, as it returns and floods the present, is sufficiently troubled. The movement of the story could be described as the central character's gradual discovery that he is an underground man, to put it mildly.

What do I mean by an underground man? A character who represents the author, perhaps, but is given no special indulgence; who reflects a lack of interest in, even an impatience with special privilege—a sense of interdependence among men—a certain modesty. The central vice of the traditional hero, who easily accepts his own superiority, is hubris, an overweening pride and expectation. The central vice of the underground man is *accidie,* moral and social sloth, a willingness to live with whatever is, a molelike inclination to accept the darkness. Perhaps these are the respective vices of aristocracy and democracy.

Among the classless men of our democracy the private detective has become a representative figure. This is true of the detectives I have known in real life as well as those in fiction. The real-life detectives imitate the fictional ones, and vice versa. Fictional detectives tend to be idealized or actualized versions of their authors: the kind of men we would choose to be if we were men of action instead of the solitary fantasists we are. Everyone knows this. What everyone may not know is that real-life detectives, both private and public, read detective stories and watch crime movies for clues as to how to conduct themselves. That's one reason why detective fiction is important: it's a model for life.

21

Eudora Welty

(Santa Barbara Writers Conference, 1977)

EUDORA WELTY is a woman who illuminates her sur-
roundings, and she does so in a quiet way, without fireworks.
Her being is as quiet and shy as the moon. Only afterwards do
you realize that the light has changed. For Miss Welty is one of
the most articulate women who has ever practiced the art of
letters in the United States. Her range of expression is remarkable, unique, extending from broad humor through tragic emo-
tion. The underpinning and undersong of all her imaginative
work seems to me to be her respect for, her fealty towards, our
common humanity. She is one of those aristocrats of the arts
who has never turned her back on common men and women.
There is a profound equilitarian and religious quality which
informs all her work and sets it apart. Miss Welty celebrates
human life in all its conditions.

This was evident in her earliest stories of Southern life which
she began to publish in the thirties. I believe she was the first
Southern writer, perhaps the first white American writer, who
was able to give her unreserved imaginative love and care to
blacks. The incorruptibility of her eye and thought is evident in
her photographs of poor Mississippi people—photographs
which have recently been compared with those of Walker
Evans in *Let Us Now Praise Famous Men*. Miss Welty took
those photographs with a plain box camera and no other para-
phernalia whatever—just the light of day and the light of her
mind.

There is no need to dwell on the long list of her accomplishments, the long list of universities where she has lectured, and the long list of public honors she has won. Miss Welty is modest to a fault. She did admit to me that in three successive days this spring she was given honorary degrees at three universities, but she would have considered it vulgar to name those universities. Still she cannot conceal the fact that her most recent and most brilliant novel, *The Optimist's Daughter*, won the Pulitzer Prize, and incidentally conferred new prestige on that award. She is an active member of the National Institute of Arts and Letters, and was given its Gold Medal in 1972.

The important thing is not the honors, but the work. Her stories are among the best and saddest and funniest in the whole range of American literature. They will never go away. She is a first-rate novelist. Her body of criticism is brilliant and still growing, in size and depth, recent additions to it being her essays on Willa Cather and Elizabeth Bowen in the *New York Times Book Review*..

I don't want to burden Miss Welty with the appellation of our best living writer. But I do suspect that, line by line, word by word, that may be what she is. She has taken possession of the language as if it were her own invention, and given it back to us refreshed, clean, brand new, with a kind of half-heard musical accompaniment, and joyous laughter in the wings.

AFTERWORD:
A Personal Appreciation

Ralph B. Sipper

I FIRST MET KEN MILLAR some time after the publication of *The Instant Enemy,* while honeymooning in Santa Barbara. What brought us together was my longstanding admiration for his work and we began to exchange letters regularly. In 1970 my wife and I established our rare book business and the relationship with Ken expanded along professional lines. He bought first editions of contemporary writers from us, not because he was a collector but because we dealt only in first editions. His interest was in text, not in notions of building a collection or of potential financial appreciation. I like to think he was helping a shaky small business venture stand on its financially impoverished legs.

Late in 1973 Ken began work on the mystery and detection anthology he edited for Knopf. Many of the books he sought were out of print and obtainable only through the offices of a book dealer. At the time, we were living in Inverness, a small town situated in the remote northwestern corner of Marin County. The mail brought his frequent requests for books by writers well-known and obscure: Queens Quorum writers, Golden Age figures, members of the hard-boiled school, minor writers whose books had been softly received. The encyclopedic range of Ken's interests defined his broad knowledge of the field and gave me my first practical demonstration of a literary expertise that extended from Shakespeare and Coleridge (on whom Ken did his doctoral dissertation) to current day literary fledglings.

We began to collaborate in matters bibliographical. I solicited his counsel concerning an elaborate book project we were putting together for the American Revolutionary Bicentennial Committee involving the choice of 200 great American works of literature. The project was stillborn, but once again the depth of Ken's scholarship proved the equal of the eminent literary scholars and professors who were on the selection committee with him.

The Ross Macdonald books we listed in our catalogues were being swallowed whole by ravenous collectors. Detective Lew Archer was getting movie and television exposure, creating even more of a demand for the books. Nor were we alone in recognizing the rare book value of Ross Macdonald's books. Dealers contacted us regularly in search of Macdonald books. Fortunately, we were in the position of getting some of an ever-dwindling supply of primary material straight from the horse's mouth so to speak.

With Ken's generous help we offered a collection of his foreign editions, more than one hundred books in some twenty languages, an impressive display of universal appeal, with imprints from all directions—Tokyo, Paris, Helsinki, Buenos Aires. The workbook and manuscript drafts of some of his books were placed at a prominent California university through our offices, so that future scholars will be able to explicate on the creative process involved in the writing of his convoluted novels.

After we moved to Santa Barbara in 1975, a PBS television movie of Ken was filmed on our premises because he felt comfortable among our book-lined shelves. He allowed me to read the working manuscript of *The Blue Hammer* and solicited my initially hesitant suggestions about it.

One fine and eventful day Ken brought Eudora Welty to the office. I had been aware of their respect for each other's work and knew they had corresponded regularly for years. Upon getting to know Eudora it was easy to see what the mutual attraction was—affinities of personality, similar qualities of grace and philosophical depth, the meticulousness with which they approached their art. It seemed to me then as it does now that Ken and Eudora view the world in much the same clear-eyed yet sympathetic manner.

By now Ken's books were universally regarded as the literature they had always been. Important critics and literary journals no longer regarded his work as genre writing. Ross Macdonald's books had burst the narrow confines of the mystery form he chose to work within. Their scope was widening. Singlehandedly, he was bringing the detective novel back to its origins—the general novel.

In publishing 24 novels Macdonald has, in typically low-keyed style, doubled the *combined* output of his early models, Dashiell Hammett and Raymond Chandler. The last dozen or so are notable for their incorporation of significant social and psychological material about the California he lives in.

The unifying symbol of *The Underground Man* (1971) is a forest fire, much like the Coyote Canyon fire that threatened Santa Barbara in 1964. An oil spill counterpoints selfish human behavior in *Sleeping Beauty* (1973), evoking memories of Santa Barbara's blackened seashore several years earlier. In *The Blue Hammer* (1976) Macdonald's concern lies with the total environment. The very first sentence finds the entire city in a state of decay. The tops of the Mission and Courthouse are obscured by smog, implying that church and state are being suffocated by careless humans who, as a direct result of their irresponsibility, are themselves finding it difficult to breathe.

The circle closes. Kenneth Millar is Ross Macdonald is Lew Archer is Kenneth Millar—man, novelist, scholar: searcher for clues to the future through unflinching investigation of the past, including his own.

ACKNOWLEDGEMENTS

"Down These Streets a Mean Man Must Go." *Antaeus*, Spring/Summer, 1977.
A Collection of Reviews. Northridge, CA: Lord John Press, 1979.
Archer in Jeopardy. New York: Alfred A. Knopf, 1979.
Lew Archer, Private Investigator. New York: The Mysterious Press, 1977.
Kenneth Millar/Ross Macdonald–A Checklist. Detroit, MI: Gale
   Research Co., 1971.
Archer at Large. New York: Alfred A. Knopf, 1970.
Find the Woman. New York: Maiden Murders, 1952.
Archer in Hollywood. New York: Alfred A. Knopf, 1967.
In the First Person (from the Davidson Films shooting script, 1971).
Writing the Galton Case. Santa Barbara, CA: Capra Press, 1973.
"Place in Fiction," *South Dakota Review*, 1975.
"A Death Road for the Condor," *Sports Illustrated*, 1964.
"Life with the Blob," *Sports Illustrated*, 1969.
Black Tide. New York: Delacorte Press, 1972.
"An Interview with Ross Macdonald," by Ralph B. Sipper, *Mystery and
   Detection Annual*, 1973.
Great Stories of Suspense. New York: Alfred A. Knopf, 1974.
"Homage to Dashiell Hammett," *Mystery Writers' Annual*, 1964.
The Writer as Detective Hero. Santa Barbara, CA: Capra Press, 1973.

BOOKS BY ROSS MACDONALD

Novels

The Dark Tunnel. Dodd, Mead, 1944. (as Kenneth Millar).
Trouble Follows Me. Dodd, Mead, 1946. (as Kenneth Millar).
Blue City. Knopf, 1947. (as Kenneth Millar).
The Three Roads. Knopf, 1948. (as Kenneth Millar).
The Moving Target. Knopf, 1949.
The Drowning Pool. Knopf, 1950.
The Way Some People Die. Knopf, 1951.
The Ivory Grin. Knopf, 1952.
Meet Me At The Morgue. Knopf, 1953.
Find A Victim. Knopf, 1954.
The Barbarous Coast. Knopf, 1956.
The Doomsters. Knopf, 1958.
The Galton Case. Knopf, 1959.
The Ferguson Affair. Knopf, 1960.
The Wycherly Woman. Knopf, 1961.
The Zebra-Striped Hearse. Knopf, 1962.
The Chill. Knopf, 1964.
The Far Side Of The Dollar. Knopf, 1965.
Black Money. Knopf, 1966.
The Instant Enemy. Knopf, 1968.
The Goodbye Look. Knopf, 1969.
The Underground Man. Knopf, 1971.
Sleeping Beauty. Knopf, 1973.
The Blue Hammer. Knopf, 1976.

Short Stories

The Name Is Archer. Bantam (1955).
Lew Archer: Private Investigator. Mysterious Press, 1977.

Essays

On Crime Writing. Capra Press, 1973.
A Collection Of Reviews. Lord John Press, 1979.
Self-Portrait: Ceaselessly Into The Past, Capra Press, 1981.

Other

Great Stories Of Suspense. Edited by Ross Macdonald. Knopf, 1974.

This first edition was printed in September,
1981 by Bookcrafters, Inc. in Chelsea, Michigan.
Body type is Trump Mediaeval set by Sun Litho
National, Van Nuys, California.